The Vagrancy P1

The Case for Measures of Restraint for Tramps, Loafers, and Unemployables: With a Study of Continental Detention Colonies and Labour Houses

William Harbutt Dawson

Alpha Editions

This edition published in 2024

ISBN : 9789362099037

Design and Setting By
Alpha Editions
www.alphaedis.com
Email - info@alphaedis.com

As per information held with us this book is in Public Domain.
This book is a reproduction of an important historical work. Alpha Editions uses the best technology to reproduce historical work in the same manner it was first published to preserve its original nature. Any marks or number seen are left intentionally to preserve its true form.

Contents

INTRODUCTION. ....- 1 -
CHAPTER I. ....- 4 -
CHAPTER II. ....- 35 -
CHAPTER III. ....- 44 -
CHAPTER IV. ....- 67 -
CHAPTER V. ....- 91 -
CHAPTER VI. ....- 104 -
CHAPTER VII. ....- 116 -
CHAPTER VIII. ....- 131 -
CHAPTER IX. ....- 140 -
CHAPTER X. ....- 154 -
CHAPTER XI. ....- 165 -
APPENDIX I. ....- 179 -
APPENDIX II. ....- 181 -
APPENDIX III. ....- 184 -
APPENDIX IV. ....- 189 -
FOOTNOTES: ....- 193 -

INTRODUCTION.

There is growing evidence that English public opinion is not only moving but maturing on the question of vagrancy and loafing, and its rational treatment. Foreign critics have maintained that we are slow in this country to listen to new ideas, and still slower to appropriate them, partly, it has been inferred, from aversion to innovation of every kind, partly from aversion to intellectual effort. If a national proneness to cautiousness is hereby meant, it is neither possible to deny the accusation nor altogether needful to resent it. Yet while this cautiousness protects us against the evil results of precipitancy and gives balance to our public life, a rough sort of organic unity to our corporate institutions and a certain degree of continuity to our political and social policies, it has also disadvantages, and one of the chief of these is that it has a tendency to perpetuate hoary anomalies and to maintain in galvanic and artificial life theories of public action which are hopelessly ineffectual and effete, if we would but honestly admit it.

The principles which underlie our treatment of the social parasite afford an illustration of our national conservatism. Alone of Western nations we still treat lightly and almost frivolously this excrescence of civilisation. Other countries have their tramps and loafers, but they regard and treat them as a public nuisance, and as such deny to them legal recognition; only here are they deliberately tolerated and to some extent fostered. Happily we are now moving in the matter, and moving rather rapidly. A few years ago it was still accepted as an axiom by all but a handful of sociologists—men for the most part regarded as amiable faddists, whose eccentric notions it was, indeed, quite fashionable to listen to with a certain indulgent charity, but unwise to receive seriously—that there was really only one way of dealing with the tramp, and that was the way of the Poor Law. That this was also the rational way was proved by the fact that it had been inherited from our forefathers, and who were we that we should impugn the wisdom of the past? And yet nothing is more remarkable in its way than the strong public sentiment hostile to inherited precept and usage which has of late arisen on this subject.

It is the object of this book to strengthen this healthy sentiment, and if possible to direct it into practical channels. The leading contention here advanced is that society is justified, in its own interest, in legislating the loafer out of existence, if legislation can be shown to be equal to the task.

Further justification this book will hardly be held to require at its writer's hands, but a few words as to its genesis may not be out of place. It is now some twenty years since I first directed attention to the Continental method of treating vagrants and loafers in Detention Colonies and Labour Houses.

Repeated visits to institutions of this kind, both in Germany and Switzerland, together with active work as a Poor Law Guardian, only served to deepen my conviction that prolonged disciplinary treatment is the true remedy for the social parasite whose besetting vice is idleness.

At the Bradford Meeting of the British Association in September, 1900, I read (before the Economic Section) a paper in which I developed, in such detail as seemed suitable to the occasion, practical proposals based, with necessary modifications, upon the result of a study of Continental methods. This paper was published immediately afterwards in abbreviated form in the *Fortnightly Review*, and was followed a little later by a second article in the same place, in which the proposals advanced were further elaborated. These proposals attracted great attention at the time; in particular they were discussed by many of the leading London and provincial journals, and it was encouraging and significant that while the novelty of the ideas put forward was admitted, they were all but unanimously endorsed by the Press and by Poor Law authorities. It is desirable to say that the first three chapters of the present book are based on, and to a large extent embody, these writings of ten years ago, though much illustrative evidence of a later date has been added; the remainder of the volume, with the exception of one chapter, although dealing with phases of the subject which I have frequently expounded before, is published for the first time.

Nevertheless, two of the pleas originally put forward have now disappeared from my argument, inasmuch as the measures to which they related have, in the meantime, been realised—one, the establishment of public labour registries, the other, the prohibition of child vagrancy, which has been dealt with in that humane law the Children Act of 1908.

As a result of the more serious attention given to the vagrancy question at that time, the President of the Local Government Board in 1904 appointed a Departmental Committee of Inquiry, before which I was invited to give evidence. The reader who takes up this book is strongly urged to study the Report of the Departmental Committee as well; it is a most able exposition of the vagrancy problem by serious investigators who were less concerned to emphasise their individual predilections than to help on the settlement of the question by uniting on broad principles of procedure. As the thorough-going recommendations of the Committee differ but slightly from the proposals which I advocated before them and here repeat, the value of the present volume will consist chiefly in the description which it contains of a series of disciplinary institutions in which other countries are actually carrying out the methods whose feasibility we are still discussing.

Pressure is happily come from other directions, and particularly from the new school of Poor Law reformers. The publication of the Reports of the

Poor Law Commission begins a new era in the history of public relief. The realisation of a constructive policy so large and fundamental as that which the Commissioners have put forward will probably prove to be the work of many years; yet whether our advance on the lines suggested be fast or slow, it must be obvious to everyone that the question of Poor Law reform is now a living one, and cannot again fall into the background.

As regards the aspect of Poor Law administration with which this volume is concerned, all those who have laboured as path-makers in this undeveloped province of social experiment must derive satisfaction from the fact that the Commission, simply endorsing the recommendations of the Vagrancy Committee, regard the disciplinary treatment of loafers of all kinds as an essential part of any reorganisation of the Poor Law. For if the deserving poor, the genuine unemployed, and the hopeless unemployables are to be treated more systematically and more humanely in the future than they have been in the past, it will be impossible to withhold from the loafers the special attention which they need.

Although the subject of vagrancy is necessarily approached in these pages from the standpoint of repression, I should feel that my advocacy had failed of its purpose if a change of the law simply stamped out the tramp without making ample provision for the *bona-fide* work seeker. I urge the abolition of the casual wards, not merely because they encourage vagrancy, but also because they are altogether unsuited to the decent workers who are on the road owing to misfortune, and not to fault. While accepting the Vagrancy Committee's conclusion that the retention of the casual wards may be necessary by way of transition, I look to the time when there will be provided for such men in sufficiency, and as part of a national system, hostels or houses of call offering on the easiest possible terms accommodation superior to that of the shelter, the doss-house, or even the so-called model lodging-house. This is done on a large scale in Germany and Switzerland, and it is little creditable to us as an industrial nation that we are so behindhand in a matter of such great social importance. The new system of labour registries, by increasing the mobility of labour, will probably help to bring home to the public mind the need for these wayfarers' hostels. With co-operation on the part of public authorities, labour organisations, and private philanthropy the cost should not prove deterrent, while the advantage would be incalculable.

January 1, 1910

W. H. D.

CHAPTER I.

THE PROBLEM STATED.

There are two large sections of sociologists who to-day strongly advocate, the one a radical reform of the Poor Law, the other the reform of the Prison system. The modern Poor Law reformer would administer public assistance with greater discrimination, showing more consideration in the treatment of the unfortunate poor, more rigour in the treatment of those whose destitution is deliberate and preventable, more care for the children, with a view to helping them past the dangers of demoralisation and lifelong intermittent pauperisation. On the other hand, the prison reformer desires to see the punitive and retaliatory aspect of imprisonment made subsidiary to the reformative, or at least he would give to the latter greater prominence than it receives at present.

Now that concerted endeavours are being made to place both Poor Law and Prison in the crucible, with a view to recasting them in new and improved forms, the time would appear to be specially appropriate for filling up an important gap in our penal system dating from the reorganisation of the Poor Law in 1834.

The reform which is urged in these pages appears to me to be the missing link in that long and unique chain of laws and orders and regulations which has in course of time been constructed for the purpose of casting round the residual elements of society influences at once repressive and benevolent, at once deterrent and remedial. While some of these elements have received attention enough—not always wise, perhaps, and often defeating its object—one element has never yet been treated rationally and systematically. I refer to the large and ever-growing class of idlers, who differ from the genuine unemployed in that they will neither seek work nor accept it when offered: the drones of the social hive, the habitual loafers.

We may distinguish in this parasitic class several clearly-defined types.

(1) There is first the type with which we are most familiar—the nomad of the highway, who is always in motion yet never gets to his journey's end, the unmitigated vagabond, who lives by begging and blackmailing and pillaging.

(2) There is also the settled, resident loafer—an urban type in the main, though the country village knows him likewise—who haunts the streets year in year out from morning till evening, living no one knows how, and whose only purpose in life might seem to be to offer disproof in his own obtrusive person of that saying of Adam Smith: "As it is ridiculous not to dress, so it is in some measure not to be employed, like other persons."

(3) There is also the intermittent loafer, three-quarters idler, one-quarter worker of a sort, and altogether good-for-nothing, who is almost invariably an inebriate and often has taken upon himself domestic responsibilities which he saddles upon the shoulders of a too-willing community—a character who mostly comes before public notice in connection with Poor Law prosecutions for arrears of maintenance.

(4) Not to exhaust the classification, there is a pitiable type for which we must go to an almost hopeless class of the other sex, a type which the Poor Law system knows likewise in connection with default in parental obligations which, but for our exaggerated notions of the limits of personal liberty, our laws would see to it were never incurred. For the virtual encouragement which the Poor Law offers to promiscuous, illegitimate, and irresponsible maternity amongst the lowest class of society should shock the sense and excite the alarm of all who are concerned for the moral and mental health of the race.

The idlers of the first two classes keep themselves most persistently before the public gaze, but in any legislative treatment of their shortcomings it is desirable that the other types should not be overlooked, and in these pages the problem of the loafer is viewed as a whole.

What society must do in its own interest, and in the interest of the idlers themselves, is to stamp out, as far as well-devised laws can do it—and we need not be too soft-hearted—the social parasite of every kind. His existence is a positive injury to the State in every way; he robs the State not only of the industry which he owes to it, but he consumes the produce of other people's labour and renders it nugatory, by abstracting from the wealth of society without adding to it; his example scandalises honest workers, for while we preach industry and thrift to the labouring classes, we assiduously foster a huge loafing class, which preaches more eloquently on a very different text, viz., that it pays best to do nothing and sponge on the community; he is a standing menace to public order and safety; and for society to tolerate him is not merely to condone, injury done to itself, but absolutely to place a premium upon social treason of a particularly insidious and vicious kind.

It is only by the veriest abuse of the modern theory of personal liberty that the Legislature, which is not slow to restrict the free action of its citizens in so many ways, has hitherto thrown a paternal and protecting arm over the loafer and the wastrel. For several generations we have done little but pet and coddle the loafer; we have treated his constitutional laziness not as the personal vice and social crime which it is, but as a venial weakness to be excused and indulged, while the man himself we have surrounded with a nimbus of maudlin sentimentality.

Think what we do for the professional idlers. Take the urban type. While honest men are working we give him the free run of our thoroughfares, and set apart for him the best of our street corners. Should he be a vagrant we make it possible for him to travel through England from the Channel to the Tweed without doing one hour's serious work save for the labour tasks which are imposed by some of the workhouses at which he may call. In these institutions—erected at intervals not too far distant to overtask his strength—food is placed before him night and morning, with a bed thrown in; while outside he can always rely upon the alms which he is able to draw from the pockets of the unwisely charitable whom he deceives with his tales of misery, or the unwillingly charitable whom he terrorises into compliance with his demands.

This was not, of course, the old English tradition. The very earliest of our Poor Laws drew a very clear distinction between the normal poor—the "aged, poor, and impotent persons compelled to live by alms," as they are described in the Act of 1530—and the idle beggar and vagabond. While provision was made for the due relief of the former, penal measures were consistently directed against the latter.[1] And when such methods of repression as the felon irons, the stocks, the whip, serfage, and transportation no longer commended themselves to the public conscience, there remained the method of summary despatch home to the town or village of legal domicile in the custody of zealous parish constables who relieved the monotony of their dignified calling with many a pleasurable jaunt over country in those old leisurely days. But the noteworthy thing about the old laws against vagrants is that their uniform purpose—whatever their effect—was not the mere restriction of this class within due numerical bounds, or the regulation of its movements within decorous limits of liberty, but its absolute extinction. In those brave days the idea of maintaining the vagrant at the public expense, and of encouraging him in idleness and vice, never occurred to the Legislature.

We have so whittled down the laws on vagrancy and idleness, however, that there are now only two ways in which it is possible to convict and punish the tramp and loafer as such. The law regards as "idle and disorderly persons" such persons, being able wholly or in part to maintain themselves or their families by work or other means, who wilfully refuse or neglect so to do, by which refusal or neglect they or their families whom they may be legally bound to maintain become chargeable to the public funds; also any persons wandering abroad or placing themselves in public places, highways, courts, or passages, to beg or gather alms, or causing or procuring children so to do, and the penalty in such cases is imprisonment with labour up to one calendar month, though should a fine be imposed instead of imprisonment hard labour must not be adjudged for default in payment. The law also regards as "rogues and vagabonds" such persons wandering abroad and lodging in any barn or outhouse, or in any deserted or unoccupied building, or in the open air or under a tent or in any cart or waggon, not having any visible means of subsistence, and not giving a good account of themselves, and the penalty is imprisonment with labour for a period not exceeding three calendar months, though on a second conviction such offenders may be imprisoned with hard labour as long as one year.

So runs the law, and in theory it does not seem ineffectual; in practice it is wholly so. For the penalties visited on "rogues and vagabonds" are virtually annulled by the care which the Poor Law has taken to allow these offenders to evade apprehension. A vagrant may be as "idle and disorderly" as he likes by day, so long as he pursues his irregular life undetected but at night he has only to present himself at the handiest workhouse, and he is forwith certified to be a deserving citizen, and is lodged and fed at the public expense.

And even about the enforcement of the penal provisions against the tramp, when his native wit and cunning fail him, and he is caught in the meshes of the law, there is an unreality and a frivolity which brings both the statute and its administration into disrepute. Nine-tenths of the "idle and disorderly persons," of the "rogues and vagabonds," who come before the justices of the peace are hardened offenders, who know more about the county gaols of the country than the most experienced of Prison Commissioners; yet the view which most commonly prevails in the police courts is that so long as the itinerant mendicant is sent on his way, and is thus got safely out of the district, expedience if not justice is satisfied. To be fair to our justices, it should be remembered that this blind-eyed administration of the law is no modern innovation. It is really only a survival of the ancient custom, already alluded to, of harrying vagabonds from parish to parish—often after a rigorous application of the whip, but in any case after a blood-curdling warning from the local justice, duly followed by a special commination from the parish constable on his own account—lest they should by any mischance fall upon poor funds to which they had no domiciliary claim. The result, however, is the same now as of old. The tramp takes his admonition, and, if need be, his punishment, with stoical indifference, and continues a tramp. The offence is condoned or corrected, as the case may be, but the offender knows that he is free to commit it again—at his peril, of course—directly the law has done with him, and that in the bathroom of the casual ward he may each evening purge the day's offences, and so begin anew on the morrow his career of licensed crime.

Who shall wonder, then, that our past indulgent treatment of the vagrant has had the effect of perpetuating and multiplying this class? The dictum of wise Sir Matthew Hale, uttered just two and a half centuries ago, is as true to-day as ever: "A man that has been bred up in the trade of begging will never, unless compelled, fall to industry."

As for the casual ward itself, it was to a large extent an accident of legislation, and certainly it was not contemplated when the Poor Law was reformed in 1834. The great constructive measure of that year, introducing the existing type of workhouse, made no reference to vagrants. The Act presupposed only the relief by the new Boards of Guardians of the settled poor. "But," the Departmental Committee on Vagrancy write, "when workhouses had been established vagrants applied for admission to them, representing themselves to be in urgent need of relief. The masters of workhouses had no means of investigating the facts and had to deal with each case on their own responsibility. At that time workhouse inmates who had no settlement were maintained at the expense of the parish in which the workhouse happened to be; this made the relief of the vagrant in the workhouse more difficult, and workhouse masters were pressed by the Guardians to refuse such cases altogether. In 1837 the Poor Law Commissioners, on being appealed to by the Commissioners of Metropolitan Police with regard to the question, expressed the opinion that it was the intention of the Act that all cases of destitution should be relieved, irrespective of the fact that the applicant might belong to a distant parish. They stated that it was the duty of the relieving officer to relieve casually destitute wayfarers and of the workhouse master to admit such cases to the workhouse. These cases were distinguished from beggars by profession, who were to be dealt with under the Vagrancy Act of 1824."[2] In 1838 the Commissioners issued instructions to the Boards of Guardians in the Metropolis pointing out their duties in regard to the relief of the casually destitute, and suggesting the adoption of arrangements for securing the performance by them of task work, and the following year a further Circular threatened with instant dismissal officers who neglected to relieve cases of urgent casual destitution. In this way the right of the vagrant to admittance became asserted: "as a class vagrants came to be recognised by the Central Authority, who from this time issued a series of circulars and orders dealing with them directly or indirectly." As a natural result between 1834 and 1848 vagrancy increased to an alarming extent in all parts of the country.

It is interesting to recall the fact that as late as 1840 the Poor Law Commissioners, though the vagrancy evil was steadily growing, were "convinced that vagrancy would cease to be a burden if the relief given to vagrants were such as only the really destitute would accept." Hence they recommended that the Central Board should be "empowered and directed to frame and enforce regulations as to the relief to be afforded to vagrants." An Act of 1842 empowered Boards of Guardians to prescribe a task of work for persons relieved in the workhouse "in return for the food and lodging afforded," though no one was to be detained against his will for more than four hours after breakfast on the morning following admission, which meant that the casual might do little or much, according to his whim. The same year the Poor Law Commissioners ordered the setting apart of separate wards for casuals, prescribed special diet for them, and regulated the task-work system. Meantime, the vagrant proved himself more and more the master of the Board of Guardians; his claim to relief having been admitted, he settled down to the view that the casual wards were convenient houses of call, intended the better to facilitate his roaming life, and this view was implicitly accepted by Poor Law authorities. More than anything else, therefore, the casual ward is responsible for the present perplexities of the vagrancy problem.

One of the first acts of the new Poor Law Board of 1848 was to inquire into the extent of the casual pauper nuisance and the causes of the abuse of casual relief; and overlooking the fact that the Boards of Guardians had been forced to accept the vagrant against their will, it blamed these bodies and told them that a remedy must be sought "principally in their own vigilance and energy." Among the measures recommended were (1) the refusal of relief to able-bodied men not actually destitute; (2) the employment of police officers as assistant relieving officers for vagrants, and (3) the adoption of a system of passes and certificates (restricted as to time and route) to be issued "by some proper authority" to persons actually in search of work. The first two of these recommendations were widely acted upon, though lack of uniformity in policy seriously hampered the efforts of those Boards of Guardians which honestly tried to do their duty.

Of the later measures introduced in the vain hope of checking vagrancy three are specially noteworthy:—

(1) A Poor Law Board Circular of 1868 and a General Order of 1871 recommending the introduction of the separate cell system.

(2) The Pauper Inmates Discharge and Regulation Act of 1871 empowering Boards of Guardians to detain casual paupers for the following times: If a pauper had not previously been admitted within one month, until 11.0 a.m. on the day following admission; if he had already been admitted more than twice within a month, until 9.0 a.m. on the third day after admission. The Casual Poor Act of 1882 extended the periods of detention as follows: First admissions during the month, until 9.0 a.m. on the second day following admission; second and further admissions during the month, until 9.0 a.m. on the fourth day.

(3) An Order of December 18, 1882, making admission to a casual ward dependent upon the order of a relieving officer or an assistant relieving officer, except in urgent cases. In effect it is well known that nearly all cases are urgent.

Considering now the extent of the vagrant population, using the term in its wider signification, and not confining it to the casual paupers[3] who are particularly enumerated in Poor Law statistics, the admission must be made at the outset that the data available are very inconclusive. It seems desirable first to call attention to the limitations of strictly official information on the subject. Since 1848 a count of the vagrants relieved in casual wards has been made by order of the Local Government Board on January 1 and July 1 in each year; since 1890 there has also been a count of vagrants relieved on the nights of January 1 and July 1; and since 1904 a count has been taken each Friday night.

According to the Annual Report of the Local Government Board for 1908 the average number of casual paupers relieved in England and Wales on each Friday night of that year was 11,491, comparing with an average of 10,401 for the year 1907; the maximum number was 13,798 on August 22 and the minimum 8,341 on July 4. The average relieved on Friday nights in London alone during the year was 1,114. A further return of the number of persons in England and Wales in receipt of relief on January 1, 1909, shows that the casual paupers numbered 15,852, 1,420 being relieved in London unions and 14,432 in provincial unions. As to these numbers, however, the Local Government Board state:—

> "These are the total numbers of casual paupers entered in the returns as relieved on January 1, 1909. The total number relieved on the night of January 1, was 9,747. To what extent the former totals include twice over persons who received relief in more than one union on the same day is not ascertainable, and it is possible that the total of the paupers relieved on the night of January 1, although omitting many casual paupers who, after their discharge from the workhouse in the morning, did not again have recourse to the Poor Law on the same day, is the more reliable."[4]

That the vagrant population, even enumerated in this partial manner, is increasing is shown by the following table, showing for a period of ten years the number of casuals relieved during day and night on January 1:—

Year	Casual Paupers Relieved.	
	At any time during January 1.	On the night of January 1.
1899	13,366	7,499
1900	9,841	5,579
1901	11,658	6,795
1902	13,178	7,840
1903	14,475	8,266
1904	15,634	8,519
1905	17,524	9,768
1906	16,823	9,708
1907	14,957	8,346
1908	17,083	10,436

It would appear from these figures that a certain relationship exists between vagrancy and trade cycles. Of the years of maximum vagrancy, 1904, 1905, and 1908 were years of more or less acute unemployment, while those of minimum vagrancy, 1900, 1901, and 1902, were years of good or fairly good trade. That the fact of an inter-relationship between vagrancy and the state of trade cannot be pressed unduly, however, is proved by the comparatively narrow limits within which, allowing for increase of population, the figures move. Certainly the figures afford no *prima facie* justification for supposing that trade depression causes any considerable number of genuine workmen to join the highway population.

Poor Law statistics, however, fail entirely to do justice to the extent of the vagrancy problem. They show the number of vagrants relieved at one time and in one way only; but all vagrants do not receive public help at the same time, and the total number on the road is far larger than the number who call at the workhouses. As to this the testimony of Poor Law Inspectors and all who have studied the vagrancy question at close quarters is unanimous. "A very large number, probably the majority, of vagrants seldom come to the vagrant wards," wrote Mr. J. S. Davy, as Poor Law Inspector for Sussex, Kent, and part of Surrey.[5] "It ought to be remembered," says another Inspector, "that the vagrants admitted to the vagrant wards represent only a very small percentage of the vagrants of the country."[6]

The Departmental Committee on Vagrancy of 1904 endorse this view:—

"The returns of pauperism published annually by the Local Government Board give figures relating to casual paupers, that is, vagrants relieved in casual wards, but these represent only a small portion of the total number of vagrants.... The vagrant is to be found in many places—on the road, in casual wards, common lodging houses, public or charitable shelters, and prisons, besides which he has many other resorts, such as barns, brickworks, etc. Then, again, the number of homeless wayfarers varies greatly from time to time, and at different periods of the year, owing to conditions of trade, the state of the weather, or the attraction of seasonal employments."[7]

Although a simultaneous census of the entire vagrant population has never been taken, certain data exist which furnish the basis for at least an approximate estimate. Several of these will be mentioned.

(1) Up to 1868 yearly returns were collected by the Home Office from the different police forces of England and Wales showing the number of vagrants of all kinds known to them. The number on the latest date, April 1, 1868, was 38,179, against 32,528 on April 1, 1867. The number of persons relieved in the casual wards of the country on January 1, 1867, was 5,027, and on January 1, 1868, 6,129, showing that the "casual paupers" at that date represented only about one-sixth of the total vagrant class. If the same proportion to population still held good to-day the number of vagrants of all kinds, based on the mean of the known number of casual paupers on January 1 of the five years 1904-8, viz., 9,355, would be about 56,000.

(2) In the county of Gloucester a count has been made for many years on a night of April of the numbers sleeping in casual wards and in common lodging houses, and the results show that the lodging-houses contain five times as many vagrants as the casual wards. Allowing for vagrants who sleep out of doors, the ratio would not seriously differ from that shown by the police enumeration already mentioned. Applying to the whole country the number of vagrants per thousand of the population of Gloucestershire, the nomad army would be shown to be 30,000. It should be remembered, however, that Gloucestershire is a county of small towns, and lies away from the great streams of population; hence it should not feel the full effect of the vagrant movement.[8]

(3) An enumeration made on March 17, 1905, by the chief constable of Northumberland, by means of police officers placed at the most important points, of vagrants on the roads between the hours of 7.0 a.m. and 7 p.m. gave a total of 300 (exclusive of Newcastle and Tynemouth), equal to about

1 per 1,000 of the population of the area covered. On this basis he placed the number of vagrants in England and Wales at 36,000. Here the omission of two important towns largely invalidates computation; their inclusion would unquestionably give a much higher ratio.

(4) A careful census of vagrants, beggars, migratory poor, etc., is taken by the police for each county, city, and burgh police district in Scotland on two nights in the year, in June and December, showing the number of these persons in (1) prisons or police cells, (2) homes and refuges, hospitals and poorhouses, (3) common lodging-houses or other houses, (4) public parks, gardens or streets, outhouses, sheds, barns, or about pits, brick and other works. The two counts of 1908 gave the following result:—

	Men.	Women.	Children.	Total.
June 21	6,815	1,843	1,541	10,199
December 27	6,129	1,391	1,541	8,506

This was equal to 2.1 and 1.8 per 1,000 of the population respectively, and if these ratios were applied to England and Wales they would represent aggregates of 76,000 and 63,000.

(5) An enumeration of homeless persons in the administrative County of London, made by the London County Council on the night of January 15, 1909, showed a total of 2,088. On that night there were also 1,188 persons in the casual wards of London, and 21,864 in the common lodging-houses and shelters, of whom 10 per cent. were supposed to belong to the vagrant class. This would give a total of 5,462 vagrants as follows:—homeless (sleeping out and walking the streets), 2,088; in casual wards, 1,188; in common lodging-houses and shelters, 2,186; total, 5,462. As the population of the administrative County of London at the date named was estimated at 4,795,757, this total is equal to a ratio of 1.14 per 1,000 of the population. The same ratio for England and Wales would give a vagrant population of about 41,000.

(6) Dr. J. R. Kaye, Medical Officer of Health for the West Riding of Yorkshire, in a report upon the influence of vagrancy in the dissemination of disease, published in 1904, estimated the roving population at 36,000. He has, at my request, explained the basis of his calculation as follows:—

> "The estimate of 36,000 refers to England and Wales, and it includes the inmates of casual wards and nomads of the same class who inhabit alternately the casual wards and the

common lodging houses according to the state of their pockets. The county police here (West Riding), make an annual census of tramps, and the figure comes out at about 1,000 persons, of whom about 200 are in the casual wards on any given night. Now the Local Government Board reports give the casual-ward population of England and Wales at about 10,000, so that if the same proportions hold good there should be about 50,000 wanderers. Or, on the other hand, if you take our ascertained 1,000 in the county area in relation to our population of 1,249,685, and apply the ratio to the population of England and Wales, we get a figure of 26,000. My figure of 36,000 comes about mid-way between the two estimates given above."

(7) A final estimate which may be quoted is that made at the request of the Departmental Committee on Vagrancy on the night of July 7, 1905, by the various police forces in England and Wales of persons without a settled home or visible means of subsistence: (*a*) in common lodging-houses; and (*b*) elsewhere than in common lodging-houses or casual wards. The result was as follows:—

(a)	In common lodging-houses	47,588
(b)	Elsewhere than in common lodging-houses or casual wards	14,624
		62,212

These totals were made up of:—

	(*a*)	(*b*)
Men	41,439	10,750
Women	4,869	2,436
Children	1,280	1,438
Children	47,588	14,624

In the opinion of the Vagrancy Committee, a considerable deduction must be made from the number returned for common lodging-houses, though, on the other hand, it appears from some of the returns that many vagrants, who would otherwise have been in tramp wards or common lodging-houses, were at the time engaged in temporary work such as fruit-picking and harvesting, and so were not included in the count. Further, an addition of about 10,000 is necessary to include the vagrants in casual wards. The Committee came to the conclusion that the census could not be accepted as "a trustworthy guide to the actual number of vagrants," and their Report contains the following guarded verdict:—

> "The number of persons with no settled home and no visible means of subsistence probably reaches, at times of trade depression, as high a total as 70,000 or 80,000, while in times of industrial activity (as in 1900) it might not exceed 30,000 or 40,000. Between these limits the number varies, affected by the conditions of trade, weather, and economic causes. In our Inquiry we are more concerned with the habitual vagrant, that is, the class whom trade conditions do not affect. Of this class there is always an irreducible minimum, though successive depressions of trade may increasingly swell the numbers. No definite figures as to this permanent class can be obtained, but we are inclined to think that the total number would not exceed 20,000 to 30,000."[9]

It may be added that the estimates of the vagrant population made by witnesses who gave evidence before this Committee ranged from 25,000 to 70,000.

The mean of all the seven estimates put forward above, as approximations only, is about 50,000, which is probably below rather than above the actual number in normal times. The estimates differ so widely, however, as to shake one's faith in the possibility of arriving at a safe figure except by a special census on even more comprehensive lines than those which underlay the Home Office enumerations up to 1868.

But even when the casual wards, model lodging-houses, shelters, and other resorts of the roaming poor have been enumerated, the full extent of the vagrant population is not told.

According to a statement made by the Prison Commissioners to the Vagrancy Committee, 3,736 out of 12,369 convicted male prisoners on February 28, 1905, were, in the opinion of the prison governors, "persons with no fixed place of abode and no regular means of subsistence"; and of 2,595 convicted female prisoners, 372 answered the same description. In other words, one-fourth of the prison population belonged at that date to the vagrant and loafing class.

The prosecutions in England and Wales for vagrancy offences in the narrower sense—begging, sleeping out, misbehaviour by paupers, and theft or destruction of workhouse clothes—fluctuated as follows during the ten years 1898-1907:—

Year.	Begging.	Sleeping-out.	Misdemeanour by Paupers.	Theft or Destruction of Workhouse Clothes.
1898	15,474	9,582	3,769	589
1899	12,659	8,515	3,632	615
1900	11,339	7,452	3,717	457
1901	14,492	9,101	5,118	576
1902	16,184	9,598	5,959	726
1903	19,283	10,349	6,496	841
1904	23,036	11,785	7,436	937
1905	26,386	12,636	6,314	1,005
1906	25,083	11,540	5,176	1,016
1907	23,023	11,164	4,633	852

At whatever figure we place the vagrant population, there is little doubt that the number tends to increase. The Vagrancy Committee frankly accept this view.

> "The army of vagrants has increased in number of late years," they state, "and there is reason to fear that it will continue to increase if things are left as they are. It is mainly composed of those who deliberately avoid any work, and depend for their existence on almsgiving and the casual wards; and for their benefit the industrious portion of the community is heavily taxed. We are convinced that the present system of treating casual paupers neither deters the vagrant nor affords any means of reclaiming him, and we

are unanimously of opinion that a thorough reform is necessary."[10]

As to the class of men who frequent the casual wards the great mass, both in town and country, are unquestionably unskilled labourers, though nearly all trades contribute a share, larger or smaller, to the sum total of vagrancy. A classification of the men relieved in the casual wards of Hitchin and Brixworth during twelve months ending September, 1906, showed the following result:—[11]

Occupations.	Hitchin.	Brixworth.
Labourers	3,830	222
Painters	226	14
Grooms	157	12
Bricklayers	144	13
Shoemakers	133	13
Fitters	123	9
Rivetters	123	—
Boilermakers	123	—
Tailors	108	5
Carpenters and joiners	106	9
Printers and compositors	74	—
Stokers, firemen, etc.	70	3
Seamen	60	4
Moudlers and drillers	58	—

Gardeners	37	—
Clerks	36	—
Engineers	34	—
Bakers	33	—
Harnessmakers and saddlers	31	—
Porters	27	—
Blacksmiths, etc.	25	—
Sawyers	25	—
Plasterers	24	—
Plasterers	22	—
Silversmiths	—	3
Other trades	446	16
Total	5,829	322

The following classification of the casuals admitted into the wards of a rural union, unnamed, is published by the Poor Law Commission:—[12]

Occupations.	1905	1906	1907
Navvies	552	772	613
General labourers	404	485	489
Carters	62	56	61

Carpenters	42	6	37
Masons	38	42	48
Grooms	37	40	60
Seamen	34	28	48
Fitters	24	—	20
Shoemakers	23	24	36
Firemen	15	21	31
Tailors	13	16	11
Gardeners	12	12	8
Miners	12	—	—
Bakers	4	13	13
clerks	11	8	38
Ironmoulders	11	5	16
Blacksmiths	9	—	13
Other occupations	142	57	69
Professional tramps	79	25	66
Total	1,512	1,610	1,673

Of 450 men admitted into the casual wards of the Skipton-in-Craven workhouse during the period September 1 to November 12, 1904, 50 were aged and infirm, while 250 described themselves as general labourers, and 150 as tradesmen.

The classification of the latter was as follows:—

Tailors	30
Joiners	15
Mechanics	12
Bricklayers	12
Painters	12
Masons	12
Spinners	12
Weavers	12
Butchers	9
Colliers	8
Printers	8
Shoemakers	8

It must be granted, of course, that every highway wanderer is not a loafer, and that the workhouse casual ward itself offers a rude hospitality to many a decent wayfarer who is deserving of a better fate, though a good deal of misapprehension exists on this subject. There is no means of learning the percentage of *bona-fide* work-seekers amongst that section of the vagrant population which fights shy of poor relief, but when one enters the casual ward it is possible at once to divide the sheep from the goats. Those who theorise upon the basis of intuition, and much more those who confuse the voting of other people's money with Christian charity, are apt to conclude that, as a matter of course, the casuals "in a lump" are not "bad," but only unfortunate, and deserve all such relief as is afforded them. It would be futile to deny to the most habitual of vagrants the power to impress even the case-hardened listener by fiction which is a good deal stranger than truth, by doubtful emotions and still more doubtful morals. Let appeal be made, however, to the trained observation of the Poor Law clerk and the weather-beaten soul of the workhouse master, and a different story will be learned. Some years ago I questioned all the Poor Law authorities of Yorkshire on the subject; half the answers placed the number of the genuine work-seekers at 5 per cent. of the whole, though in special cases a much higher percentage was allowed. The Vagrancy Committee, on the evidence placed before them, estimated the proportion of genuine work-seekers at 3 per cent. of all casual paupers.

These figures are in keeping with all we know of the experience of the Poor Law Inspectors who report from year to year to the Local Government Board upon the vagrancy question. To quote one opinion only by way of illustration:—

> "The more I see of the vagrant class the more strongly I am impressed with the conviction that the number of those really in search of work is relatively very small. Over and over again I have gone into the casual wards and have, in answer to my question, been told by the vagrants that they were all seeking work but could not find any; but when I have pointed out that farmers were everywhere advertising for hands, they had nothing to say, except, perhaps, that farm labour did not suit them. In the agricultural districts it may be said, generally, that enough labourers can rarely be obtained, and the local newspapers are scarcely ever without advertisements for them. No doubt some of the able-bodied paupers know nothing of farm work, and if they can be enticed to labour colonies, which would teach them, agriculture may gain, but there is a large demand for absolutely unskilled men which they refuse to supply. For example, last summer, a tradesman in a small town in Somerset asked the master of the workhouse to send him half-a-dozen labourers, to whom he would give permanent employment for 18s. a week. Six of the occupants of the casual wards professed themselves as eager to accept this offer, but, on leaving the workhouse in the morning, all but one slipped away. That one remained, and has been earning his 18s. a week ever since, but the other five have presumably found begging more profitable."[13]

The Local Government Board, as we have seen, have endeavoured to check vagrancy by urging Boards of Guardians to adopt the cell system, and to impose upon the casuals systematic labour tasks proportioned to the frequency of their visits. Yet though the cell system has been pressed upon workhouse authorities since 1868, so far only two-thirds of them have adopted it. As to the labour task, the Local Government Board advise that vagrants should, as a rule, be detained for two nights and required to perform a full day's work, but that the period of detention should be extended to four nights in the case of those who seek admission twice within the same month.

There is no general practice to this effect, however, for every union follows its own devices for making the life of the tramp hard or easy as the case may be, and in the absence of a uniform policy, few unions take the question of vagrant regulations seriously. The average Board of Guardians attacks all its problems on the line of least resistance, and the line of least resistance in dealing with the tramp is to follow the advice of the incomparable constable Dogberry, and get him out of sight as soon as possible, thanking God that it is rid of a knave.

The reports of Poor Law Inspectors have for years abounded with complaints of absence of uniformity in the treatment of vagrants and of the evil results of the existing state of anarchy. To quote several of recent date:—

> "While many unions have adopted the Local Government Board's suggestions, others have ignored them. It is useless for one union to take steps for driving casuals away from their workhouses simply to plant them on others."[14]

> "There is a want of uniformity as regards detention and the task of work in the various casual wards, and it is worthy of notice that at Loughborough, where the guardians, after a short trial of two nights' detention, decided to revert to a one night's detention only, the number of vagrants has increased from 10,751 in 1906 to 12,058 in 1907."[15]

> "There is a great want of uniformity in the treatment of vagrants as regards accommodation, detention, diet and tasks of work, and guardians are naturally averse to taking any action involving expense pending legislation on the subject."[16]

> "Some mitigation of the evils of vagrancy might be possible if guardians fully exercised the powers possessed by them. No uniform practice prevails. The system of a two nights' detention, with the imposition of an adequate task, is uncommon in this district. Some kind of task is prescribed in the majority of vagrant wards, but for the most part vagrants are released the following morning after admission. Here and there the regulations are enforced with

beneficial results. Guardians are, perhaps, apathetic or disinclined to detain more often, because they are not enabled to deal effectively with this class owing to insufficient accommodation. A system of two nights' detention, combined with proper discretion and supervision on the part of the workhouse master, has generally been followed by a diminution in the number of vagrants, but an absence of any such similar practice in neighbouring unions largely defeats these good results. Vagrants simply avoid these wards, and pass on to those where the restrictions are less severe."[17]

As the Departmental Committee on Vagrancy say:—

"It is much easier for a workhouse master, or the superintendent of the casual ward, to allow vagrants to discharge themselves on the morning after admission without labour, than to detain them, and insist upon their doing the regulation task of work, and the discretion which is left to the officers with respect to the discharge of certain classes of vagrants results in a complete variety of practice."[18]

Again:—

"Where a union carries out the regulations as to detention and task of work there is always a reduction in the number of admissions to their casual wards, but the evidence before us shows that severity of discipline in one union may merely cause the vagrants to frequent other unions."[19]

In London, according to the evidence given before that Committee:—

"Some guardians do not detain, some give one task, some another, and some practically none at all.... Some Boards of Guardians say the casuals are working-men honestly looking for work, and there is no doubt they are, but they know where they are going to get it. When they leave, they know to what casual ward they are going, and whether they are going to break stones or pick oakum. The consequence is, that the London vagrants flock to Poplar, Thavies Inn, and the other wards where detention and work are not enforced, or where only a light task is given."[20]

All experience shows that the frequency with which vagrants visit given parts of the country is in exact proportion to the comfort or otherwise of the casual wards, and a change either way means a difference in the number of loafers entertained. "If a tramp likes the ward he is there again within the month, and perhaps in a fortnight," was the verdict of a witness before the Poor Law Commission.

"The slightest relaxation with reference to the quantity or quality of food given in workhouses leads immediately to an increase of vagrants," writes a Poor Law Inspector.[21]

Another Inspector, explaining decreases in the numbers of vagrants in some of his districts, says:—

> "A small cause will apparently divert the vagrant stream from its usual course. Where a change of master has taken place, or where gruel has been substituted for bread and water, or *vice versa*, there has frequently occurred, very rapidly, a large increase or decrease in the numbers applying for admission to the casual wards where these changes have taken place."[22]

An illustration of tramp susceptibility to the attractions of the dietary is related by the Poor Law Inspector for Cumberland, Lancashire, and Westmorland, as follows:—

> "In 1908 ... the guardians of the Leigh Union decided in the autumn to make an improvement in the dietary at their casual wards, a proceeding in which they did not invite the co-operation of other Boards of Guardians. The result was an influx of vagrants into the union, which swamped the accommodation, and rendered administration impossible. The admission to the Leigh casual wards for the first six months of the year had shown an increase of 33 per cent., as compared with 1907; in the second half of the year, the comparative increase was 164 per cent. The comparative increase for the latter half year in Lancashire as a whole was under 30 per cent., and none of the unions adjoining Leigh showed an increase greater than 60 per cent."[23]

Only those who have had practical experience of Poor Law work know how fastidious the tramp is in the choice of his involuntary tasks. In connection with the casual wards of a Board of Guardians of which I was for many years a member the task imposed was breaking 13 cwts. of stone. We added to this task the riddling and wheeling away of the stone. The result was that many tramps would come to the door, read the regulations, and walk off, while others, who entered and asked what they would have to do, would at once leave with "No, thank you." Several tramps resolutely argued the illegality of the extra task with the master, and tried to evade it.

It may be said that the case advanced against the vagrant up to this point rests upon negative grounds. Even were he an idler and a parasite and nothing worse, however, he has no claim to be tolerated. Those who tell us that vagabonds and loafers form, after all, an insignificant proportion of the population, and that the Poor Law holds out severer problems for our solution, forget or undervalue the fact that every one of these people is a centre of moral contagion. To ignore them because they are a small minority in society is just as rational as it would be to ignore gangrene because its effects are local only, or a plague because its victims are as yet few in number. Each of these loafers creates imitators. On the highways he is a walking advertisement of the advantages of idleness; in the model lodging-house, the night shelter, the wayside inn, he acts the part of recruiting sergeant for the great army of sloth and vice.

The vices of the vagrant, however, are by no means all of a negative order. From the standpoint of public security and order it is intolerable that the known criminals, which the majority of tramps are, should be afforded every facility for following their irregular calling. Incidents like the following, cited at random, are of weekly and almost daily occurrence in all parts of the country, and bring home better than argument the folly of our present method, or lack of method, of treating the tramp and loafer:—

> "An attack on a lady in a lonely country road, between the Potteries and Leek, has been reported to the local police. The lady, who lives near Dunwood Hall, had been visiting an invalid, and on her way home was waylaid by a tramp, who attempted to rob her. A severe struggle took place, during which the lady was viciously handled. In the end the tramp was frightened by something and decamped."

> "At the Mansion House, a plasterer was charged with vagrancy and assault. On Tuesday night the prisoner knocked at the door of St. Mary Aldermary Rectory, and applied for assistance. The rector's butler, after consulting the rector, told him to go away, whereupon he struck him in the mouth, cutting it, and loosening two of his teeth. The rector went to his man's assistance, and the prisoner placed himself in a menacing attitude and attempted to strike him, saying that he would have his rights. The prisoner placed his shoulder against the door and prevented it being shut. Ultimately he was given into custody.... Sentenced to six weeks' hard labour."

The reports of Poor Law Inspectors frequently illustrate this aspect of the vagrancy problem. To quote from one only:—

> "Another aspect of vagrancy, peculiar to rural districts, is the sense of insecurity which is created in the minds of people living in remote localities. Sometimes methods of threats and intimidation are resorted to to enforce demands when it is safe to do so. Truculent and insubordinate, as is proved by his frequent appearances before the magistrates for refusing to perform his allotted task, he is a burden to the community, and a nuisance alike to the police and to the Poor Law authorities."[24]

The laxity with which the law against mendicancy is enforced is notorious, and upon this question also the reports of Poor Law Inspectors contain interesting reading. "It is impossible," wrote Mr. J. S. Davy several years ago, "to deal adequately with the question (of vagrancy) without having regard to the mode in which the police carry out their obligations under the statute, and the action of magistrates when vagrants are charged before them. There are obvious difficulties in the way of the police laying too much stress either on the apprehension of beggars or the prevention of sleeping out, and these difficulties affect magistrates, who occasionally discourage the police from proceeding against offenders under the Vagrancy Act."[25]

Another Poor Law Inspector wrote in 1906:—

> "With regard to the punishment of vagrant offenders, it is very unfortunate that there is so little uniformity in the sentences in Leeds. While the stipendiary magistrate gives, as a rule, lenient sentences, the West Riding magistrates deal more rigorously with those who come before them. There seem to be no fixed principles governing the cases."[26]

The following extract is taken from a Yorkshire newspaper of April, 1903:—

> "Three labourers of no fixed abode (it is the police constable's well-known euphemism for a vagrant), were charged at Skipton with begging at Kelbrook. The prisoners fairly took the village by storm. They were singing and shouting, and swore at women who would not relieve them. One of them kicked a door, and their conduct generally was altogether disgraceful. After they had collected 3½d., they went to the public-house and asked to be supplied with a quart of beer for that amount. The girl who was in supplied them for the sake of quietness, and after drinking the beer the men went out, collected the same amount, came back,

and demanded another quart for 3½d. The men were sent
to gaol for fourteen days each."

Very outrageous, of course, yet very common, and also very natural. For given the implicit licence to beg, why not give the tramp also the licence to spend the proceeds of begging in his own way, and if he gets drunk and is violent, is it not the fault of those who furnished the money? But "fourteen days!" There is the true irony of the incident. For the same men probably served fourteen days a month before, and would serve fourteen days a month later, since the vagrant's time is notoriously divided pretty equally between the gaol and the highway. If, however, our penal laws are intended to be not merely punitive, but also, and mainly, reformatory, a system which consists of sending men into and out of prison at more or less regular intervals is obviously futile and childish. It is the obligation to work which these men, and tens of thousands like them, need to come under. Dislike of regular labour makes them tramps, tramping makes them criminals—the two conditions are inseparably connected as cause and effect, for their kinship lies in the very constitution and instincts of human nature, and the police laws which ignore it are engaged in an encounter from which they must of necessity emerge foiled and beaten. They may hide the tramp for a time from view, but they will not cure him; the very iteration of the futile penalties which are imposed upon him only confirms him in the conviction that vagrancy, mendicancy, rowdyism, and blackmailing are venial offences, the commission of which society almost takes for granted, since it has arranged that they may be compounded for upon terms so easy as to amount to open incitement to illegality.

"Evidence is available on all hands, both from magistrates and from those connected with the administration of the Poor Law," the Vagrancy Committee of the Lincolnshire Quarter Sessions of 1903 write, "that the present short-term sentences, especially in view of the improved prison dietary, are a treatment of no deterrent value.... If the present methods are not deterrent, the evidence is also clear that neither are they reformatory. If the man *bona-fide* out of work and seeking work be excluded, a very large proportion of those convicted for vagrancy are found to be habituals. Many of these cases are either mentally or physically below the normal standard, and it is obvious that such cases cannot be successfully dealt with during the very short periods for which they are brought under the prison influence."

The Committee cite one notorious case in which between December 8, 1881, and October 23, 1903, a period of under twenty-two years, a man of thirty-seven years had been sentenced to imprisonment thirty-one times in Lincolnshire, and after he had done all continued an unprofitable servant. His sentences were as follows:—

Sentence of seven days   5 times

"   ten days   2   "

"   fourteen days   9   "

"   three months   12   "

"   six months   1   "

"   twelve months   2   "

An interesting feature of these sentences was the way in which shorter and longer sentences alternated. In another case a man of thirty years had been sentenced twenty-three times within five years, *viz.*, between July 14, 1898, and June 29, 1903, as follows:—

Sentence of seven days   6 times

"   ten days   3   "

"   fourteen days   4   "

"   one month   2   "

"   six weeks   1   "

"   three months   5   "

"   six months   2   "

To quote the words of the Prison Commissioners:—

> "The elaborate and expensive machinery of a prison, whose object is to punish and at the same time to improve by a continuous discipline and applied labour, cannot fulfil its object in the case of this hopeless body of men who are here

to-day and gone to-morrow, and who, from long habit and custom, are hardened against such deterrent influences as a short detention in prison may afford."[1]

Moreover, our medical authorities are at last on the track of the tramp, and none too soon, for several recent epidemics have convinced them that he is one of the most proficient disseminators of disease. The following incidents, all relating to the last wide-spread epidemic of small-pox, are typical of his services to society in this respect:—

> [27]"A tramp who was making his way through the Lake District was found lying by the roadside near Ullswater on Sunday evening in an advanced state of smallpox. He was removed to a smallpox hospital, and it was ascertained that he had been infected by another tramp, who is now in the Penrith Hospital." (*March 5, 1903.*)
>
> "At Northwich three more begging cases were dealt with. The chairman said tramps were mainly responsible for the smallpox prevalent in the district. Cheshire was infested, and if vagrancy could be put down they intended to do it."
>
> "Smallpox has broken out in a somewhat serious form at Barking, and several families have been removed to the isolation hospital. The outbreak is attributed to a tramp, who was found lying in the roadway at Ripplesdale with a severe attack of the disease."—(*May 19, 1903.*)

How disease is disseminated by tramps is graphically told in the following newspaper paragraph relating to the epidemic above referred to:—

> "On December 20, 1902, a tramp named —— entered Doncaster Workhouse. He said he came from Worksop way; had been sleeping out; had not had any food for three days; and complained of aches and pains all over him. He was isolated as much as possible in an end ward of the Workhouse Infirmary. On December 26, he was found to be suffering from small-pox, and immediately removed to the Small-pox Hospital. Four inmates who had been in contact with the case were isolated and re-vaccinated, and a nurse, also re-vaccinated, was told off to attend to them, and not allowed to go near the other inmates.
>
> "On January 8, a second case of small-pox occurred in the workhouse. This inmate, it appears, had sorted the clothing of the first case. He complained of illness on January 4, and developed the disease on January 8. The amount of trouble

that was given in isolation, re-vaccination, and disinfection must have been very considerable, and must all be debited to the tramp who introduced the disease."

The report for 1903 of Dr. J. R. Kaye, the West Riding of Yorkshire Medical Officer of Health, stated:—

"Yorkshire towns have had such a visitation of smallpox, that we read with interest the part played by the tramp genus in spreading it. Last year there were 144 cases of the disease in the West Riding. In nearly every centre affected, the tramp was responsible for its introduction. Thus we find at Keighley, where the greatest number of cases occurred, the infection was brought by a man who had been 'on tramp' seeking employment. The 15 cases at Barnsley were attributed to tramps of the lodging-house class. A recent investigation has shown that out of 138 towns having cases of small-pox, in no less than 100 its introduction was attributed to persons of the same class. At Sheffield, out of 28 importations, 21 were brought about by tramps, and at Huddersfield, 8 out of 13 invasions were traced to similar channels. It is significant, that in districts away from the main roads trodden by these nomads, small-pox was unknown. Clearly something will have to be done with this highly objectionable person if we are not to have small-pox always with us."

In a paper on "Tramps and the Part they Play in the Dissemination of Smallpox," read in July of the same year at the Sanitary Institute's meeting, Dr. Kaye said:—

"In the recent prevalence of small-pox, some 12,000 cases have occurred in the provinces (since January, 1902), and experience all over the country shows that the most subtle agency of distribution is not to be found in the close commercial intercourse of our communities, but in the wanderings of the relatively insignificant number of people whom we designate tramps."

As a result of the discussion which followed, it was resolved to request the Government to "take into consideration the necessity for legislation to deal more effectually with those resorting to common lodging-houses and workhouse tramp-wards, as a constant and dangerous element in the propagation and dissemination of smallpox."

The following year Dr. H. E. Armstrong, Medical Officer of Health for Newcastle-upon-Tyne, published an elaborate report on the same epidemic, based upon inquiries addressed to the Medical Officers of Health throughout the country. As a result of the epidemic, which began in the latter part of 1901, and lasted the two following years, 25,341 cases occurred. As to their origin, Dr. Armstrong came to the following conclusions:—

> (1) Of the 126 districts from which returns were received, 111 had been invaded by small-pox in the epidemic, and in 57 or 51 per cent. of these, the disease was first introduced by vagrants. In 25 of these latter districts spread of infection from vagrants occurred.

> (2) Small-pox was introduced secondarily by vagrants into 58 districts, and, perhaps, into two other, at least 305 times. Such secondary introductions of infection took place with the following frequency:—

Number of Times Infection was Introduced.	Number of Districts.
1	11 or 12
1 or 2	1
2	11 or 12
3	5
4	5
5	3
6	3
7	2
8	7
9	7
9 or 10	7

11	7
12	7
13	7
23	4
24	4
31	4
34	4

(3) It was found that the vagrants were housed in the workhouse in 41 districts, and in common lodging-houses in 58. The number of cases of small-pox occurring in these lodging-houses was 'at least 606,' and probably more, though 19 districts reported that the disease was introduced into common lodging-houses (169 with 165 cases) otherwise than by vagrants.

(4) In 35 districts there was reason to believe or suspect that infection had been carried elsewhere by vagrants leaving those districts—in most cases twice or more.

(5) Infection was first introduced by vagrants into 58 per cent. of the 63 large towns to which the inquiries extended, and was carried sooner or later into 72 per cent. of these towns, and on an average about five times to each. The disease had been taken to 30 workhouses and about 70 common lodging-houses, causing a large number of fresh cases, but had been of comparatively slight prevalence in such houses when not brought there by vagrants.[28]

So, too, at the meeting of the Sanitary Institute, held on February 7, 1903, at Manchester, Dr. E. Sergeant, Medical Officer of Health to the Lancashire County Council, reported that "The spread of smallpox was owing most largely to the vagrant class," and he claimed that "these parasites should not be allowed to go about the country spreading disease, and it was very little to ask that they should be vaccinated," for it seems that under present legislation, while the parasite can require you to support him, you cannot require him to protect himself, much less you, against infectious disease!

Furthermore, guardians of the poor have become increasingly alive to the fact that one of the most difficult tasks which they have hitherto had to discharge, in the administration of the existing law, will compel them before long to face this wider problem: I refer to the question of child vagrancy. For oftentimes the tramp has both wife and children, and unless a benevolent public interposes and relieves him of their maintenance, they accompany him on his wanderings. Passing over the humane aspect of the question, I would ask: What does this ghastly parody of family life mean? It implies that where there is one vagrant now there will in all human probability be two, three, four, a few years hence. Calling attention to the fact that during the year 1908 3,899 children were admitted to vagrant wards, the Report of the Local Government Board remarks:—

> "Debarred from education and all that is essential to the formation of settled habits, they are subjected to great hardships, and it would be strange if, under such conditions, they did not become bound to the road."[29]

Our forefathers recognised three and a half centuries ago that vagrancy was hereditary, for an Act of 3 & 4 Edward VI. (1550), reciting that "many men and women going begging carried children about with them, which, being once brought up in idleness, would hardly be brought afterwards to any good kind of labour or service," gave *carte blanche* to any person willing to appropriate such children and bring them up to honest labour till the age of eighteen years if boys, or fifteen if girls. It may be said that this was legalised kidnapping, and that our modern way of dealing with the children of tramps is better. For we have got so far as to recognise that the liberty of vagrant parents to drag their offspring round the country is a vicious liberty, and should not be tolerated, though we are not agreed on preventive measures. The Poor Law Acts of 1889 and 1899 empower Boards of Guardians, under certain specified circumstances, to assume and exercise parental rights over the children of pauper parents, and the Children Act, 1908, prohibits child vagrancy under penalty, and makes provision for placing in public or other suitable custody the children of persons who are unfit to discharge parental duty.[30] These statutes do not interfere with parents' liability to maintain their children, though in other hands, yet the enforcement of that liability will prove difficult, if not impossible, in the case of a vagrant. Unless such a parent voluntarily abandoned a roaming life, the Poor Law and police authorities would have to choose between the alternatives of perpetually chevying him from pillar to post or letting him go scot free. Obviously, legislation which leaves the question of parental responsibility in so unsatisfactory a position cannot be the final word on the child vagrancy problem.

Viewing the question of vagrancy from all sides, we shall be compelled to endorse the verdict of the Lindsey Quarter Sessions Committee:—

> "The cost to the community of this class is immense, for they produce nothing, they necessitate large additions to our workhouses, involving heavy cost to the rates, and they overcrowd our prisons. At the same time they form a ready recruiting ground for the criminal classes, they are a continual nuisance to rich and poor alike, and they leave behind them families worse than themselves."

CHAPTER II.

THE URBAN LOAFER.

The vagrant is only one type of social parasite, however, and in some respects he is not the most obnoxious. When we leave the casual wards and enter the workhouses themselves, a further loafing element confronts us, adding to the difficulty of our problem. For though these institutions nominally exist for the reception of people who are not only destitute but are unable to prevent their destitution, we find that the able-bodied pauper is to a large extent in possession.

It is interesting to recall the fact that when workhouses were established, the tendency which the Poor Law authorities fought against was, that the aged and infirm of the labouring class regarded them as infirmaries for their permanent maintenance. A Report of the Poor Law Commissioners of 1840 protested against the idea that workhouses should be placed on the same footing as almshouses.

"If the condition of the inmates of a workhouse," they wrote, "were to be so regulated as to invite the aged and infirm of the labouring classes to take refuge in it, it would immediately be useless as a test between indigence and indolence or fraud—it would no longer operate as an inducement to the young and healthy to provide support for their later years, or as a stimulus to them, whilst they have the means, to support their aged parents and relatives. The frugality and forethought of a young labourer would be useless if he foresaw the certainty of a better asylum for his old age than he could possibly provide by his own exertions...."

Nowadays, the difficulty of Poor Law Guardians is to prevent, not the aged and infirm, but the middle-aged and able-bodied from making the workhouse their permanent home.

"Once admitted into the workhouse in England," says the Majority Report of the Poor Law Commission, "the pauper is usually left undisturbed, the Guardians seldom exercising their power of discharge." This generalisation is unjust, yet what is said certainly holds good of a large number of workhouses. While, however, Boards of Guardians are mainly to blame, the laws which they have to administer are also, in part, responsible. In the absence of institutions for the detention of loafers such as exist in Continental countries, these loafers are able to abuse the Poor Law at will, and snap their fingers at the police. Within the workhouse they are a cause of perpetual annoyance, and their presence and example are a fruitful source of demoralisation and disorder.

Speaking of this class of able-bodied paupers in relation to the Sheffield Union, Mr. P. H. Bagenal, Poor Law Inspector for the West Riding, reports:—

> "The master states that this class gives infinite trouble. They have no fear of prison; in fact many of them prefer it, and state that the work is not so hard and the food better. Many of them have got good trades, such as fitters, plumbers, builders, iron workers, etc., and could earn from £3 to £4 a week if they chose. They prefer to go to the workhouse, where, however, they only work under compulsion, and give all the trouble they can to the officers."

Commenting upon the fact that of the persons relieved in England and Wales during the year ending September 30, 1907, 26,179 had been relieved five times or more, the Poor Law Commission state:

> "The number of persons ascertained to have been relieved five times or oftener during the year shows the existence of a troublesome class who make a convenience of the workhouse, and whose improvidence is born of the knowledge that that institution is always at hand."[51]

The Poor Law Inspector for the Metropolis relates that, as a result of a call-over of the 900 inmates of a London workhouse in 1907, it was found that fifty able-bodied men and fifty-three able-bodied women were among them. The Committee reported:—

> "In a large number of these cases there did not seem to be any tangible reason why they were in the workhouse at all.... Many admitted that they had done no work for years; in fact could not give the date or place where they had last worked. Many of this class were so reduced in physique on admission that they could not be classed as able-bodied, but with the regular diet and absence of intoxicating liquors they rapidly recovered; but unfortunately for the worst classes the conditions of the house appear to be conducive to their disinclination to shift for themselves.
>
> "Upon such cases again coming before the committee, it was found that several inmates, who appeared to be quietly settling down for the remainder of their lives, had awoke to the fact that the guardians were making investigations, and had taken their discharge."

The Committee were also impressed by the number of men who

> "When their wives refused to keep them longer, and as some of them openly expressed it 'the wife turned me out,' came to settle down in the house—in many cases drink and desertion were found to be the causes of the wives' action."[32]

Mr. Lockwood, another Poor Law Inspector, stated before the Poor Law Commission:—

> "Probably, if it is an overcrowded workhouse, it is impossible to prevent the able-bodied class from sharing in the comfort, and I may say the luxuries of the older ones.... You cannot prevent that class finding the conditions of life in a mixed workhouse such as they are not entitled to, and ought not to share in."

Another witness, speaking of the Marylebone Workhouse, said:—

> "The association in large numbers in the able-bodied blocks becomes an attraction; and it appears to me that some method of breaking up such associations, accompanied by systematic training under healthy conditions, would be advantageous.... The master feels very strongly that what the men require is to be given continuous work, which they are able to do, and to be separated the one from the other. They regard the workhouse as a kind of club house in which they put up with a certain amount of inconvenience, but have very pleasant evenings."[33]

It was stated that the Marylebone workhouse deals with 300 of these men every week.

The master of the Bethnal Green workhouse confirmed what has been said. "This class of man," he said, "is well known to the master of every London workhouse as the able-bodied loafer. As a rule he is a strong, healthy fellow, knowing no trade, having a great dislike to work, and possessing all the attributes of the soft-shelled crab, willing to live upon the fruits of the labour of the worker, so long as he can avoid the sharing of responsibility himself. There is no doubt that the moment this man becomes an inmate, so surely does he deteriorate into a worse character still. Unless rigorously dealt with and made to work under strict supervision, he has a fairly good time in the house, and after a month or so he has mastered every trick of the trade, and becomes a confirmed in-and-outer, taking his day's pleasure by giving the necessary notice, and returning the same evening more contented than ever with his lot in the house. Something for nothing is degrading the man, until all of the manhood has left him, and there remains for the ratepayers to keep an idle, dissolute remnant."

To quote another witness, who referred specially to the Poplar Union:—

> "The pauper in the workhouse intends to be there; he is either going to be there or in some other institution all the days of his life. My experience is, that the average have been in from ten to twelve years, and some of them nineteen years, and they are young men now. The workhouse is no deterrent to any man. It simply harbours them, and as long as the workhouses exist, these men will exist."

Similarly, the report of the Stepney Guardians for 1908 states:-

> "There are too many opportunities in a general workhouse for the vicious of both sexes to meet. The dining hall and other parts of the workhouse common to all classes afford means of communication—generally of an evil character. It is no uncommon event for a man and woman to strike up an acquaintance in a workhouse, which ultimately results in increased burdens on the ratepayers. Messages are conveyed, *billets doux*, ill spelt but tender, are exchanged; an assignation is made, resulting in the amorous couple leaving the workhouse together when, dispensing with the blessing of the Church on their union, they tramp the countryside as man and wife during the summer months. At the approach of winter the man returns, with a sigh of relief, to his old bachelor quarters in the workhouse, where the gleeful account of his exploits is listened to with open-mouthed admiration by the youthful male pauper, and with envy by the hoary sinner. In this manner, a feeble-minded woman and a physically enfeebled man—both chronic paupers and chargeable to this union—begat five children, all of whom were born in the workhouse, and were reared at the expense of the ratepayers."

The same testimony comes from rural districts. "It is certain," Mr. B. Fleming, the Poor Law Inspector for Dorset, writes, "that the tendency has been to induce the loafer class to think that they would have provision made for them, and that therefore they need not trouble much about it for themselves."[34]

Writing of the "in-and-out" class of workhouse inmates, the Poor Law Commissioners say:—

> "It is not too much to say that this class has been created by our administration of the Poor Law, while the law itself affords no means of checking it now that it has come into existence. These are the men and women who frequent the workhouse for short periods, often taking their families with them, and are constantly taking their discharge. They go out when they want more licence, and return when they need to recruit themselves after a debauch."[35]

Moreover, the married urban loafer, like the married vagrant, inflicts incalculable injury upon others. While it has been made a misdemeanour to drag children round the country, the pauper of the "in-and-out" type can still with impunity commit a crime no less outrageous upon the offspring for whose decent maintenance he is legally and morally responsible. For the children of such intermittent paupers are introduced to workhouse life and breathe the atmosphere of pauperisation from their earliest consciousness. When the father enters the house, the children go with him, and for them, as for him, life is an alternation of abject dependence and equally abject liberty.

"Through these children," says the Report of the Poor Law Commission truly, "the evil (of pauperisation) is being perpetuated to another generation, for they get no chance of education, while they become habituated to constant appeals to the Poor Law, and lack the advantages of either home or school life."[36]

As a Poor Law Guardian, I had to do, on one occasion, with an able-bodied pauper of this kind, who, on the ground of destitution, obtained admittance to the workhouse with his large family. Once in, he was so satisfied with his new surroundings and freedom from responsibility, that for many months it proved impossible to dislodge him. Under the master's eye he was willing to do the work required of him, but he had no wish to find employment outside, and did not leave the house until he was literally ejected.

It is true that the Poor Law Act of 1899 gives power to Boards of Guardians to appropriate neglected children, and so preserve them from the ill effects of their vicious training.[37] That is undoubtedly kind to the child, and in the end it is bound to be advantageous to the public. But here comes in an absurd anomaly: Whatever the theory of the law may be, we practically leave it to the option of the parents to evade responsibility or not as they will. All they have to do is to make themselves scarce, and the Poor Law officials and the police may find them or they may not. I know of one Union in whose workhouse there are, at the moment of writing, six children of one father, and he an able-bodied man, who has fled from the district once, and only refrains from doing so again because he knows that he is under strict police supervision. Rousseau deposited his offspring on the steps of the Foundling

Hospital at dead of night, and went away, thinking noble thoughts, for this was a part of the harmonious "Social Contract," and everybody else could do the same. The English loafer yields his children to workhouse care with but the gentlest pretence of unwillingness, and betakes himself to liberty, lightened of a disagreeable burden, and reflecting that of all strange devices for relieving him and his kind of parental responsibility and of encouraging the multiplication of paupers, the Poor Law is the strangest.

Prosecution for maintenance, if the offender can be found, and a short imprisonment if he refuses to pay, are the corrective measures already available against the parents who culpably transfer their parental liabilities to the public, and over 3,000 convictions are registered yearly by the courts for neglect to maintain family.[38] It is notorious, however, that proceedings of this kind are taken by Poor Law authorities reluctantly, since the magistrates in many districts habitually stretch the law in favour of defaulting parents. What we should do, and shall have to do, in such a case, is to take the loafer, too, and after disciplining the idleness out of his nature, give him back his family obligations, and see that he discharges them.

Furthermore, in all large towns a considerable proportion of the frequenters of the casual wards are not even *bona-fide* vagrants, but simply idlers of the locality, who, so long as these refuges exist, feel no disposition to work and establish homes for themselves. Of the men admitted to the casual wards of the Manchester and Chorlton Unions in a certain year, no fewer than 4,000 were found on analysis to belong to the neighbourhood. The experience of Birmingham is to the same effect. Of the London casual it has been said:—

> "He is in most cases a loafer who simply migrates from one ward to another. He is in Whitechapel to-night, and in St. George's-in-the-East to-morrow night, and he will go across to Kensington the next night, but he does not leave London.... They have their times for excursions, when they go either to the seaside or hop-picking or fruit-picking, but for the greater part of the year they are in London, and they circulate round about the casual wards."

The number of admissions to the Metropolitan casual wards in 1907 was 196,470; the number of separate individuals was not known, but 18,009 persons were identified as having been admitted more than once during a month. The Report of the Vagrancy Committee states, indeed, that 98 per cent. of the persons admitted to the casual wards of London are loafers. A witness stated before that Committee:—

> "They are not working men. If you give them a job for a day or two days perhaps they might do that, but you must not expect them to work longer; they do not like working longer than a day or two.... A lot of them are young fellows. If you could get hold of them when first they come into the casual ward and get them away, something might be done."[39]

By way of substantiating the foregoing statement, it may be recalled that of 689 casual paupers prosecuted at the Metropolitan police courts by the Poor Law authorities in 1907, 538 or 78 per cent. were charged with refusing or neglecting to work.

The indulgent spirit in which the urban loafer is regarded in this country is well illustrated by the free hand given in London to the army of work-shirkers and unemployables, irrespective of nationality, to take possession of the public streets for the purpose of demonstrations in every time of acute unemployment. A large number of the men who paraded the streets on the latest occasion of the kind were unquestionably deserving men, who would have accepted any work offered to them, but the vast majority were notoriously only unemployed because they had neither desire nor intention to be otherwise. "Those who are not loafers are worse," was the verdict of a police inspector who had scrutinised one of the processions; "there are very few genuine unemployed among them; most of them never did a day's work in their lives," and another police officer, who analysed a procession at my request, assured me that he knew every man, and not one in fifty would ever do a day's work if he could help it. It was even worse with the London "unemployed" processions of the early months of 1903. When these were in full progress, the Chairman of the Wandsworth and Clapham Board of Guardians wrote to *The Times*:—

> "The superintendent of the casual wards at our workhouse has had opportunities this week of seeing the processions of the so-called 'unemployed.' He assures me that he detected amongst the number several hundreds who habitually came before him as vagrants, and it is his opinion, after consultation with others holding similar positions to his own under the Poor Law authorities, that 80 per cent. of those who are allowed to parade the streets belong to the casual class."

At a meeting of the Strand Board of Guardians it was reported that "hundreds of the processionists were tramps and workhouse inmates, who had asked leave to look for work and took part in the march so that they might spend their share of the collection in beer." From first to last these demonstrations were organised and engineered by socialistic agents, who called the tunes and paid the pipers generously so long as the public provided the necessary funds. Beginning with a couple of men and a collecting box, they expanded on the snowball principle day by day, until they numbered hundreds of men and scores of collecting boxes, and at last created a street scandal which was daily anticipated with mixed curiosity, disgust, and alarm. There was never any spontaneity about the processions; agitators fixed the rendezvous, marshalled their hosts, conducted the tours, and paid the demonstrators so much per head for the walk round, according to the proceeds of the collecting boxes. So far did the farce go, that police constables were at last told off to assist the loafers to perform their perambulations with due convenience and order. And these bands of "demonstrators," composed of such elements, had the audacity to go through the solemn farce of passing deliberately drawn-up resolutions day after day, protesting that owing to the selfishness of the propertied classes they were doomed to lives of "compulsory idleness," and calling on the Government to adopt measures to remove the "state of famine in time of peace" from which they suffered!

It was quite in keeping with the absurdity of the whole proceedings that a strike of the processionists, caused by a deduction from the day's pay by way of contribution towards the expenses of the show, should have threatened the collapse of the parades long before the philanthropy of the spectators was exhausted. And yet while this wholesale begging was condoned by the police authorities, and carried on with their help, isolated mendicants were all the time pursued with the customary rigours of the law. "At the North London Police Court," ran a newspaper record, while the processions were at their height, "a costermonger was sent to twenty-one days' hard labour for begging as one of the unemployed. He admitted that he had hitherto been in organised processions, but thought he would do better by begging alone. A gaoler stated that he had known the prisoner for many years, and he seldom, if ever, did any work."

Happily, although public convenience suffered, public security was not seriously threatened during those eventful days, when, out of sheer jealousy lest the sacred principle of the "liberty of the subject" to do what he likes should be infringed, the authorities, day after day, handed over the principal thoroughfares of the Metropolis to a mob, whose will to create anarchy was probably only checked by its physical inability. Under the same favourable circumstances, a well-fed mob might have placed London, for a time, under a reign of terror.

What the intelligent foreign observer thinks about English town loafers, and the indulgent way in which we humour their weaknesses, may be judged from the following reflections of a recent German visitor to London:—

"When the Londoners say, 'These are our unemployed,[40] they do not see what strikes a foreigner at once—that all these dirty, ragged figures do not give the impression of out-of-works at all—that they look rather like people who endeavour to keep miles away from work. No man who really wants work looks like the average London unemployed. He has no time to lounge at street corners or patrol the principal streets—which are certainly not places where work is to be found. Doubtless there are thousands of genuine out-of-works in London, but these are not the people whom the foreigner sees.

"The foreigner naturally asks: How do these people live? And the answer makes him acquainted with an English institution which is probably unique of its kind in the whole world—which is certainly unknown to the German: it is the 'workhouse.' The name recalls our own house of correction, but the 'workhouse' is in fact the opposite of that. As a rule, it is a fine building—in Lambeth we might almost call it a palace—to which every man who is out of work has access. There he receives supper, bed, and breakfast, after which he is able to go in search of work again. If he finds none he may return to the workhouse in the evening, and, as one might expect, this is what he generally does.

"The workhouses are maintained at enormous cost, and it is characteristic of the good heartedness of the Englishman—for the Englishman is good hearted—that he pays this cost, out of local taxes, without grumbling. That the institution is a wise one, however, I doubt. The man who says to himself that he must have sixpence or he will have nothing to eat to-morrow will go to far more trouble to get these coppers together than the one who says: "At the worst I can go into the workhouse."'[41]

CHAPTER III.

DETENTION COLONIES AND LABOUR HOUSES.

In whatever direction we look, misguided indulgence is seen to be shown to classes amongst the least deserving in the community. But our systematic playing with this question cannot relieve us from the duty of facing it in all its seriousness, and of adopting whatever measures a due consideration of public policy may suggest.

I come, then, to the question of remedies. What can, what should, be done? Shall we, in despair, settle down to the conviction that the loafer is not to be extinguished, but must be regarded as filling an inevitable, though not, of course, a desirable, place in society? Or shall we try to exterminate him by the expedient of compelling him to perform the social functions which alone establish for him or for anyone a right to any place in the commonwealth? I take the latter view, and I base my contentions upon the maxim of Stuart Mill—no unreasoning advocate of interference with personal freedom:—

> "Whenever there is a definite damage, or a definite risk of damage, either to an individual or to the public, the case is taken out of the province of liberty and placed in that of morality or law."[42]

To the proposals originally put forward so many years ago, I return with increased conviction, not only of their practicableness, but of their urgency; with the assurance, moreover, that public opinion now fully recognises their reasonableness and necessity. Proceeding from the presupposition that the maintenance of vagrants at the public expense is contrary to sound economic law, to the common interest, and to commonsense, I contend that the status of vagrancy should be made in reality, what it is already in theory, illegal. That principle admitted, the task which remains will be less to do away with the vagrant than to make the vagrant do away with himself. To do this will entail no revolutionary change of the law; on the contrary, it will only be necessary to put into operation, seriously and systematically, the law as it exists at the present time.

And first I would lay down as a foundation principle, as the starting point from which all reformative measures must proceed, the transference from the Poor Law to the Penal Law of the entire tribe of loafers who systematically abuse public relief—the vagrant of the casual ward; the shirker of domestic responsibilities, who throws his family upon the Union and absconds, or who sneaks into the workhouse on every possible pretext, dragging wife and children with him; the drone who makes periodical visits to the labour yard; and the able-bodied pauper whose destitution is due to intemperance or an otherwise irregular life.

To the Poor Law and to Poor Law institutions people of these classes emphatically do not belong, and all past failure to make the slightest impression upon them is in my opinion primarily due to the persistent mistake of treating their case as coming under the law of public charity—a mistake which is also a wrong so long as the idle poor are maintained, in any degree whatsoever, at the expense of the industrious poor.

The practical measures which would be needful are these.

(1) In the first place, let loafing of every kind, and not merely the loafing of the casual pauper, be made a misdemeanour. For if we begin to exterminate the idler of the highway, we must, in fairness, deal with his kinsman of the street and of the workhouse.

(2) In sympathy with this measure, restrict the right of free migration in the case of the destitute unemployed to the extent of making it dependent on permission to travel in search of work. (The man with money in his pocket is his own master all the world over.)

(3) Further, and particularly, abolish the casual ward, as we logically must do. This may seem a strong measure, but so far as the tramp is concerned, it is really the fulcrum on which the lever of reformation must rest. "The why is plain as way to parish church." If vagabondage is to be regarded as an offence to be punished instead of an innocent weakness (which it never was and never can be) to be humoured, then the vagrant's free lodging-house must disappear. It is obvious that so long as we maintain wayside shelters for the special reception of tramps, it will be hopeless to repress vagrancy. The casual ward invites vagrants and creates them. Moreover, it is entirely incompatible with the laws which already exist for the nominal repression of vagrancy. It is illegal to beg, it is illegal to wander about without means of subsistence, but there is no habitual vagrant living who is not guilty of this compound fracture of the law, and few who have not been punished for it. Nevertheless, we wink at these misdemeanours, and in housing some 10,000 vagrants every night in the casual wards, we offer direct encouragement to known law-breakers to persist in illegality.

(4) But at these negative and repressive measures it will be impossible to stop. Their very operation would compel us to go further, for the tramp and the loafer having been hustled from their wonted haunts, and the casual ward having been shut in their faces, they would either have to betake themselves to honest work, or they would fall into the hands of the police, either as mendicants or homeless wanderers.

Here is seen the need for a new departure in our penal system. At present no correctional institutions exist suited to offenders whose radical fault is constitutional idleness. Discipline, enforced by all necessary use of compulsion, is their principal need, and this discipline can only be given in special institutions.

The ordinary prison has proved its uselessness for the treatment of the vagrant and loafer, for not only has it failed as a reformative agency, but its life has no terrors for him. By the testimony of prison governors and magistrates, the tramp, on the whole, prefers the prison to the present workhouse; an institution that would exercise a deterrent influence must, therefore, offer a severer discipline than either.

Complaint was made by the Standing Joint Committee of the Lincolnshire magistrates some time ago that mendicancy had increased 100 per cent. on account of the superiority of the prison dietary. "The professional tramp," said one magistrate, "was no fool, and he very much preferred in many instances to go to prison than to enter the casual wards of the workhouse." The Lindsey Quarter Sessions Committee appointed in 1903 to consider the question of vagrancy reported:—

> "Frequent cases have come to the knowledge of the Committee in which tramps in the casual wards, when threatened with prosecution before the magistrates as a consequence of a refusal to work, have openly avowed their preference for prison life, and cases are also noted where, after sentence, the prisoners have made a similar statement as to their having no dislike for prison. This failure, they believe, is also partly due to the changes in the form of the 'hard labour' enforced, due to the abolition of tread wheel, crank, etc. Owing to the difficulty of arranging suitable work, and to requirements of the prison for chapel, meal hours, marching to and from work, etc., the hours of actual labour, as well as the severity of the work available, bear no comparison with those of many kinds of free labour outside. Prison conditions, indeed, to many persons with so low a standard of physical comfort as the average vagrant, must be extremely comfortable and even attractive."

Evidence to the same effect might be cited in abundance from other quarters. The point is one to which the Departmental Committee on Vagrancy gave special attention. Asked by the Committee "Do you not find that the seven days' sentence given to these tramps induces many of them to commit some small offence to get imprisonment, with a view to being helped along by rail to their destination?" Lieut.-Col. J. Curtis Hayward, Chairman of the Gloucestershire Vagrancy Committee, replied:—

> "I do not think the prison has any terror. For instance, in one union they have had a great number of cases of refractory tramps, and they have always stated, when they have been had up, that they would rather do the hard work in prison than break stones in the workhouse, because it is easier work. I have been told by the governor of a gaol that some of the prisoners said that they liked the fare better than they did that of the workhouse."

Another witness, before the same Committee (Mr. A. C. Mitchell), speaking for Wiltshire and Gloucestershire, said:—

> "I think that under present conditions the sending of vagrants to gaol is utterly useless. They want to go to gaol; the conditions in gaol are better than those in casual wards, and particularly in bad weather they prefer going to gaol. Over and over again it has come before us: a man commits some petty offence in order to go to gaol for a short period."[43]

What are needed in this country are the Detention Colonies and Labour Houses[44] which have long been provided in Continental countries for this type of offender. To these institutions, differentiated according as they were intended for hopeful or for incorrigible cases, all vagrants and loafers should, after due warning, be committed for a period sufficiently long for disciplinary purposes.

Besides being penal in character, these institutions might also offer, under suitable conditions, a temporary home to unemployed persons of all kinds. It might be objected that this would be a practical admission of the principle of the Right to Work. For myself I do not care much for phrases, but even if this should be the case, I would reply that the Right to Work is an infinitely better and wiser and safer principle to concede to the masses than the Right to be Idle. And yet the admission of the Right to Work would be no new thing in this country. It was enacted as early as the fourteenth century, in a Poor Law of 12 Richard II. That law drew a distinction between "beggars impotent to serve" and "beggars able to labour." The former were "continually to abide during their lives" in their native towns, or wherever else the enactment of the statute happened to find them, and the latter were to be given work suited to their strength and capacity. It may be recalled, too, how this same principle was carried further by the Poor Laws of Elizabeth's reign.

It follows that the Detention Colonies and Labour Houses, by offering admission to unemployed persons willing to enter voluntarily, would allow Poor Law authorities to abolish the labour yards for test work. Few Poor Law workers defend these yards, which under the existing law are flagrantly abused by local able-bodied loafers.

Forced labour for the loafer is still more an English tradition, though, like the Right-to-Work principle, long disregarded. The Act of 27 Henry VIII. (1535) enjoined local authorities, besides maintaining the impotent and aged poor:—

> "To cause and to compel all and every the said sturdy vagabonds and valiant beggars to be set and kept to continual labour, in such wise as by their said labours they, and every one of them, may get their own living with the continual labour of their own hands."

The cost of these institutions was to be defrayed by alms collected by the churchwardens and others, but any parish which neglected to carry out the Act was liable to a fine of 20s. for every month of omission. The Act of I Edward VI. (1548) contained similar provisions. Early in the reign of Elizabeth a proposal was laid before the Government by a Somerset justice of the peace for the erection of houses of correction, adjacent to gaols, for the reception of convicted vagrants, who should be there "kept in work, except some person would take them into service," and, added the memorialist, "I dare presume the tenth felony will not be committed that now is." An Act of 14 Elizabeth (1572) empowered the local justices to use surplus monies collected for the relief of the impotent poor in putting rogues and vagabonds to work in "convenient places," under the control of the overseers. A more systematic plan was that proposed by the Act of 1575, requiring Quarter Sessions to establish "abiding houses or places convenient in some market town or corporate town or other place," to be called houses of correction, and to be stocked with wool, hemp, flax, iron, or "such other stuff as was best suited to the country" (*i.e.*, the locality), with implements for the manufacture thereof, and in these houses were to be "straitly kept, as well in diet as work, and also punished from time to time," vagrants and beggars, and other people of questionable utility to the commonwealth. The Act threatened with a fine of £5 every justice who left Quarter Sessions "before conference had touching the execution of this statute," the fines to go towards the cost of establishing and furnishing the houses of correction. Similarly, an Act of 1597 required the justices to provide houses of correction for vagrants to be used in addition to the county gaols. In 1609 an Act was passed exposing to a penalty of £5 every justice of a county in which a house of correction was not provided within two years. These institutions were established on a considerable scale, but in course of time their reformative purpose gave place to a penal one. As the Vagrancy Committee point out:—

> "In 1630 a Royal Commission, issued for the purpose of enforcing the vagrancy laws, directed that the houses of correction should be made adjacent to the common gaols and the gaoler made governor of them, so that the prisoners in the gaols might be taught to work as well as those committed to the houses of correction. After this date the houses of correction seem to have been regarded more and more as places of punishment, to which persons were committed for definite terms to do hard labour, rather than to be taught to work; and in many counties the common gaols were used as houses of correction. It is from an amalgamation of the two that the modern local prison has sprung."[45]

Throughout the following century the tendency to regard vagrancy less from the standpoint of public safety and policy than from that of public expense gained the upper hand. Vagrants, as such, had ceased to be obnoxious; what was disliked was their propensity for throwing themselves upon the charity of parishes in which they had no settlement. Hence the policy of whipping these offenders, whether women or men, and restoring them to their legal parishes, was consistently followed in the eighteenth century. It was an irrational and costly policy, though in keeping with the particularist spirit of the times. In 1821 a Select Committee of the House of Commons was appointed to consider the abuses which had arisen out of this system of "passing" vagrants, and, as a result, the existing legislation on the subject was repealed in 1822. It was stated in the House of Commons at that time that in Wiltshire and an adjoining county £2,587 had been expended from the county funds in one year in "passing" vagrants and that in 1821, £100,000 had, in the aggregate, been spent in this way.

Nevertheless, that the idea of curing the loafer by forced labour was not entirely forgotten, is proved by the fact that in 1848, when the Poor Law Board took the place of the Poor Law Commissioners appointed under the Poor Law Act of 1834, a proposal to return to the old disciplinary method was put forward by one of the first Poor Law Inspectors, Mr. Aneurin Owen, who recommended the establishment of pauper depots on islands off the coast, at which local stone might be broken for road use.

I confess to attaching more importance to the disciplinary influence of rigorous restraint, coupled with active exertion, than to any number of periodical months in county gaols. Punishment may do good or may not: but punishment is not enough. It is not—in the main, at any rate—a dangerous criminal class with which we have to do, but for the most part the weak and aimless characters whose great need is the moral tonic of discipline and compulsion. Lodged in such institutions as will be described in later chapters, these evaders of all social obligations would learn, or at least would be taught, both how to work and the duty of industry. As I shall show, Belgium, Holland, Germany, and Switzerland have all found it advantageous to establish Labour Houses, true to their name, for the special treatment of social parasites of this kind, and while imitation in details may be neither possible nor desirable, their experience throws valuable light upon both sides of the problem—on the one hand, the case of those hardened offenders upon whom indulgence is thrown away and, on the other hand, the case of the budding loafers who have not irrevocably chosen between the life of diligence and that of sloth.

The possibilities of the philanthropic Labour Colonies of the Continental pattern, to be conducted by Boards of Guardians, have impressed many Poor Law reformers who have begun to occupy themselves with the tramp. I may claim to know well the work of the best voluntary Labour Colonies of the Continent, having visited some of them, and while agreeing that institutions of this kind—albeit with the addition of compulsory powers of detention, which the Continental colonies do not possess—might do for young and first offenders, I am confident that a *régime* many degrees stricter and more methodical would be necessary before they could hope to make any impression upon the habitual loafer. Here, however, we see the idea of coddling the tramp, even while we are trying to reform him, creeping in already in a new guise. These good people readily admit that discipline of some kind is necessary; but while they would restrain the tramp henceforth, it would be with cords of love. The poor fellow has been taught by the rude buffeting of the workhouse to hate labour. Who would love work after he had, for years, been passing through the mill of the casual ward, which grinds the instinct of diligence and self-respect slowly, indeed, but exceeding small? This has been the hard experience of the tramp. The continual sight of heaps of stones and oakum, which he was expected to disintegrate according to their kind, by way of paying for his humble bed and board, has created in him a distaste for even more dignified kinds of labour, so that the very sight of a spade, a pick-axe, or a dirty apron gives him quite a turn. So the tramp's tender-hearted, ever-faithful sympathisers are arguing; he shall not be passed under draconian laws if they can help it.

There can be no hope of advance on the right lines until this mischievous appeal to sentiment is abandoned. It has been the bane of the Vagrancy Laws for generations, and more than anything else is responsible for the present difficulties of the tramp problem in its several phases. Short of compulsion, the tramp will not work, and the hope of inducing him to take to a life of industry, by placing him in an atmosphere of art and poetry, perfumes and texts, is to go counter to all the lessons of experience, and to utterly misunderstand the instincts of the tramp nature. Else how explain the notorious fact that wherever a workhouse adopts a fairly severe labour test there the tramp cannot be persuaded to go; while, conversely, the easier the terms of admission—or, more truly, of exit—the fuller is the casual ward. I read in the newspapers, at the moment of writing, that "The new labour tests adopted by the Sleaford Guardians are answering very satisfactorily, and at the fortnightly meeting, the master reported that during the past six months there had been a decrease of 250 vagrants at the Union." The fact that this official had also to complain of "dissatisfied vagrants," and "the breaking of windows and other Union property" by these irreconcilable visitors, only confirms the truth that vagrancy and hatred of work are convertible terms. But, if so, it follows that it is only by curing this unsocial aversion to exertion that the unsocial practice of vagabondage will cease to perplex and scandalise society, and to do that, coercive measures of a very definite kind will have to be employed, let the repository of power be as it may. The treatment of the tramp must, of course, be humane—that it should be other is inconceivable in these days, when even the inmates of our prisons are assured a standard of life far beyond the reach and hope of thousands of the poor who help to maintain the prisons and the prisoners—but it must, none the less, be distinctly punitive and deterrent. It must not be desirable to be sent to a disciplinary establishment of this kind; a man must rather be willing to work voluntarily outside than to work compulsorily inside.

In addition to those sentenced to detention for vagrancy, the forced Labour Houses would meet the case of several other classes of notorious delinquents. They include the following:—

(1) Husbands who desert their families, and against whom legal redress cannot be obtained.

(2) Paupers of the "in-and-out" class who use the workhouse as a means of evading their parental responsibilities.

(3) Able-bodied paupers whose destitution is due to idleness and unwillingness to maintain themselves.

(4) Dissolute persons whose life is an alternation of more or less regular work and spells of indulgence from which the workhouse is their only hope of recovery.

(5) Certain classes of confirmed inebriates.

(6) Unmarried women of inferior mental and moral capacity, dependent on the rates, who have had more than one illegitimate child.

Some of these offenders would be committed by the magistrates owing to the action of the police in the ordinary way. In Poor Law cases it would be justifiable to dispense with open judicial proceedings, and to empower the Poor Law Authority to commit, on a certificate signed by one or more magistrates, giving the offender (as in Hamburg)[46] the right of appeal, first to the authority itself against the execution of its resolution to proceed, and before the execution of a magisterial certificate to Petty Sessions.

There remains another class of persons who constitute a serious social burden and inconvenience, the criminals, loafers, and paupers of alien origin, who probably are more numerous, and certainly are more indulgently treated, in England than in any Continental country. At present a small minority of the criminal aliens convicted are deported after the completion of their sentences. The number of aliens (the Colonies and India not counted), convicted and committed to the local prisons in 1907 was 2,799, or 4.3 per cent. of the total number. The aliens recommended for deportation in that year numbered 289.[47] It is conceivable that deportation will be resorted to upon a very much more extensive scale, and eventually that the duty and expense of punishment, where the alien is detained, will be undertaken by the country of nationality; there is obviously little reason or satisfaction in maintaining criminal aliens in prison when banishment awaits them immediately on release.[48] As for the alien vagabond and loafer we have the example of Continental States to guide us. The laws of Germany, Austria, Belgium, and Switzerland expressly enjoin expulsion as the treatment of such persons; they are simply taken across the nearest frontier, and are warned against returning. It would not be unreasonable to apply to alien loafers the summary treatment which their own Governments do not hesitate to enforce. As to the destitute who fall upon the Poor Law, it should be possible to conclude with Continental Governments treaties applying internationally the principle of "relief settlement," under which each State would either receive its own citizens who became chargeable to the public funds of another country, or at least would refund the costs of their maintenance to the Poor Law Authority which discharged this duty for it.

The latest complete return of alien paupers in England and Wales relates to July 1, 1903, when their number was 1,753, of whom 897 were relieved in London, and 856 in the provinces. They included 587 indoor paupers, 694 outdoor paupers, and 472 insane in asylums. Exclusive of the insane, they consisted of 117 men relieved with wives or children, 95 wives of men relieved, 95 women relieved with children, but not with husbands, 362 other men, 193 other women, 359 children of men and women relieved, and 60 other children. Of the total of 1,753 alien paupers of all classes, 715 or 41 per cent. were from Russia and Poland, 502 or 30 per cent. from Germany, 110 or 6 per cent. from France, 106 or 6 per cent. from Italy, 70 or 4 per cent. from Norway and Sweden, and the remaining 250 represented twenty-three other countries. In London the aliens represented 0.74 per cent. of the total pauperism, in the provinces they represented 0.33 per cent. The support of these outsiders constitutes a public burden for which there seems no moral justification. The question of their treatment is one which should not be approached in a captious, much less a bigoted, spirit, but if it is inequitable—as the law declares it to be—that one English Poor Law Union should support the paupers of another, it is doubly inequitable that the nation should show to other countries an unequally reciprocated generosity in the care of so many of their citizens, and these amongst the least desirable.

It would be essential to success that detention should, in all but the most hopeful cases, be for a long period. This is not only the practice of all Continental Labour Houses, but the past prison treatment of vagrants in this country proves the uselessness of short sentences. In Germany the term of commitment may extend to two years; in Belgium it must fall within two and seven years. At the same time discretion should be given to the authorities to curtail the sentence, within fixed limits, where the detainee gives proof of reformation and a desire to follow a regular mode of life. In such a case, release would be on parole, and in the event of a repetition of the offence which entailed commitment, the man would be reapprehended and sent back to the Labour House to complete his sentence without further legal procedure.

There are strong reasons why Detention Colonies and Labour Houses should be county institutions, just as they are provincial institutions in Prussia. The fact that many of their inmates, under the organisation proposed, would be defaulters committed on the application of the Poor Law Authorities, is a strong argument for such a local basis. There is reason to fear that if the Colonies and Labour Houses were formally incorporated in the prison system of the country, they would imbibe too much the prison atmosphere and spirit, and would tend to become identical with existing houses of correction, just as the houses of correction of the sixteenth and seventeenth centuries ultimately lost their special character as reformatory institutions. It might be desirable that offenders sentenced should be removed for detention to the county in which they had legal settlement, in preference to being punished in the county in which the offence was committed, but failing that course, the county or parish of settlement would be liable for all costs of maintenance as in the case of non-settled paupers.

While primarily the cost of these institutions would be a county charge, Poor Law Authorities would be required to pay on a fixed scale for the maintenance of all persons detained at their instigation, and it might be expedient to require in respect of every detainee a certain contribution from the parish in which he had legal settlement, as is the case in some of the Swiss cantons. The liability of the detainees themselves would be compounded by their labour, which it would be the business of the Colonies and Labour Houses to employ to the best possible advantage. Although, on this plan, the institutions would be under county management, it would be necessary that the State should exercise far-going powers of control, either through the Home Office, the Local Government Board, or the Prison Board, and that all schemes of organisation, regulations, the more important appointments, and also expenditure of certain kinds, should receive the approval of the Central Authority.

It should not be required, nor would it be necessary, that every county should have its own Detention Colony or Labour House. For reasons both of economy and efficiency counties would be allowed to combine. Only in this way would it be possible to secure variety of type in the establishment of these institutions. Not much experience would be needed to show that the same treatment would not suit every class of offender; most of the Colonies, no doubt, would be fairly uniform, but one or more would be required for the more rigorous discipline which would have to be meted to old offenders. Possibly, a single Colony of this kind, organised after the pattern of the Beggars' Depot of Merxplas, in Belgium,[49] would serve for the whole country. If the existing Poor Law is, in the elegant phrase now current, to be "broken up", it might be found that some of the existing rural workhouses would serve as the nuclei of Detention Colonies of the milder type.

It would be a condition of establishing Detention Colonies and Labour Houses, that they should exist for the purpose of hard work, for the art of labour is only acquired by labour. Of such work the average loafer is quite capable, if only the necessary pressure could be applied. As to vagrants, official statistics show that the majority of them are in the able-bodied period of life: of 5,579 casual paupers relieved on January 1, 1900, about 70 per cent. were between thirty-five and sixty-five years of age; 23 per cent. were between sixteen and thirty-five years, and only 5 per cent. were above sixty-five. If the vagrant can, every day, walk the almost incredible distances which he tells us, there is in him immense store of energy which is going to waste. A Detention Colony, properly organised, and infused with an atmosphere of industry, would use this energy for the good of society and of the loafer himself.

It would be judicious, as well as equitable, to pay the detained worker wages, or a bonus on output, by way of encouraging him to diligence and exertion, and of providing him with decent clothing, tools, and a small sum of money wherewith to begin life again on regaining his liberty. Even the most conscientious of free workmen is spurred by the thought of the wages which will reward his efforts, and there is nothing ignoble in such a stimulus. The natural atmosphere of a Detention Colony is that of the outside labour market, to which, by right, the detained workers belong, and the existence of a money nexus between the man and his work will be a set-off against the chafing thought of bondage, a constant reminder that the man, in doing well for the colony, is also doing something good for himself, and an incentive to those habits of honesty and application which will alone enable him to regain, and permanently retain, control over his own life. Moreover, the wages or bonus should be held before the worker in the clearest and most definite manner—not as an act of charity, but as a "business proposition," not as largess, but as a right. If the man can be incited to a healthy egoism, so much the better; he will be the less likely to fall back when he has to fight his way outside. In short, payment should be an essential part of Detention Colony policy, and the moral value of the habit of money earning should not be spoiled by too much talk of privileges and favours. The character of the Colonies and of their inmates, the unfavourable conditions under which much of the work would have to be done, and the limited market that would be available for its produce, would necessarily restrict the wages to a very small sum; the essential thing is that they should be paid, and that the workers should be able to estimate the amount of their possible gains beforehand.

It would seem expedient that every Colony or Labour House should follow a mixed economy of agriculture and industry. Wherever possible, a farm should be an essential part of it, in order that all such primary necessaries of life as milk, butter, meat, roots, and vegetables, might be produced, as far as practicable, by the aid of the inmates' labour. It would also be advantageous, following the example of the Voluntary Colonies which have been established in this and other countries, to begin each settlement on a tract of land, a considerable part of which, at least, is undeveloped, with a view to the provision of an abundance of rough outdoor labour by means of works of reclamation, and to securing to the Colony the increased value which such works would create. It is also desirable that the Colonies, while lying away from towns, should have good means of communication.

On this subject some words may be quoted from a letter recently written to me by Monsieur Louis Stroobant, the energetic director of the Belgian State Beggars' Depot at Merxplas:—

> "It is expedient to create establishments like Merxplas in districts but little populated and situated at some distance

> from towns. It is also indispensable that a colony of this kind should be near a small railway station or a canal, in a healthy country, should be well provided with drinking water, and should be in a locality in which the inmates would be able to make the bricks needed for buildings."

While, however, farm and land labour would form an essential source of employment and of gain in the Detention Colonies, the broad basis would need to be industrial. This is proved by the experience of all the forced Labour Colonies of the Continent of which I have knowledge, with the one exception of the Rummelsburg Labour House, near Berlin, and in this exceptional case the labour of the inmates is largely used in working the extensive sewage farms of the Berlin municipality. For obvious reasons, it would be necessary to choose such trades as could be carried on economically. In the first place, comparatively few men of the type suited to a Vagrant Colony are fit for ordinary farm work, which needs far more skill and intelligence than most urban advocates of Labour Colony schemes seem to imagine. After allowing for the relatively small number of inmates whose labour would be needed on the farm all the year round, the remainder, the great majority, would have to be employed on works of improvement, and in the workshops. The former work would necessarily be of an intermittent character, and even so would, in time, be reduced to very limited proportions. Unless outdoor employment altogether outside the establishment, such as road-making, draining, levelling, gardening, and forestry, were to be resorted to, as in some of the German forced Labour Colonies, it would be necessary to fall back on industrial work. Probably it would also be found that training in such work would offer most men the best chance of reinstating themselves in society when they obtained their release, and from the financial standpoint it would undoubtedly yield the best results for the Colony.

The question of allowing the products of Detention Colonies to compete with the products of free labour would inevitably arise, and not improbably the bare possibility of such competition occurring would be used as an argument against the establishment of these Colonies. It is obvious, however, that if the object of Detention Colonies is to assist their inmates to go back into the world able to earn an honest livelihood by industry, there must be some slight sacrifice of private interest to public advantage. Clearly, a policy of give and take would have to be adopted. There are products which forced Labour Colonies might legitimately be allowed to send into the open market without injury to the most sensitive outside industry—farm produce, for example, if a superfluity were available—but, as far as possible, the goods produced should be for home consumption and for the public services, as is the case in other countries. The interchange of products between the various Colonies should be encouraged, as it would not only lighten the common burden of maintenance, but would facilitate trade specialisation and the classification and grading of the inmates.

It would be unwise to hope, however, that any Labour Colony would be made self-supporting, in spite of some confident opinions to the contrary which were put before the Vagrancy Committee. The very fact that the Colonies would have to be worked with an inefficient class of labour, and the inevitably high costs of administration and oversight, make it impossible to regard them as profit-earning institutions. Nevertheless, if a Colony were well organised, well managed, and not too tightly restricted in the character of its industries and the extent of its market, the costs of maintenance should not be heavy. In this respect the experience of the Belgian and some of the Prussian and Swiss Labour Houses, dealt with later, is very encouraging.

More important than any consideration of immediate financial results, however, is the permanent influence of Colony discipline upon the inmates; if that were assured, financial success would also be certain, if not to the Colony itself, then to the community outside, which is practically the same thing. It is imperatively necessary, however, that we should at the outset be perfectly clear, not only as to the object aimed at in setting up Detention Colonies, but as to the practical possibilities of these Colonies. The object must not and cannot be to make perfect men out of most imperfect material; it will be the far more modest one of correcting tendencies of character and conduct which are socially injurious, with a view to returning the objects of care to freedom, if they seriously wish to regain freedom, able, under favourable circumstances, to take an independent place amongst the social hewers of wood and drawers of water. Only by setting before ourselves sane and moderate views shall we be working to serious purpose; to act otherwise will be to waste effort and court certain disappointment. It is hardly too much to say that it will be safer to aim too low than too high in undertaking the difficult task of socialising and moralising the loafer.

Let us indulge in no illusions on the subject: the proportion of the detainees who will be really "reformed" will be exceedingly small; those upon whom some wholesome influence, of longer or shorter duration, will be exerted, will form a larger number; but it is possible that the great majority will return again and again to detention and may even prove irremediable and entirely unfit to be restored to society.

In the main, therefore, the Detaining Colonies may, in the end, prove to be largely institutions of restraint. Yet even on that basis they are necessary, and the service which they will do to society will by no means be a negative service. They will, in fact, be carrying out the idea which more and more finds favour amongst penologists, and which must inevitably be far more rigorously applied in the future than it is now, that persons whose liberty is injurious to the commonwealth must be deprived of that liberty, permanently if necessary, and in any case so long as they continue capable of social harm.

It may be asked, can a place be found in a system of Detention Colonies and Labour Houses for the Voluntary Labour Colonies and Depots of various types which already exist in this country? To my mind, the latter would still be able to do a most important and indispensable work, and to do it under conditions more favourable to successful results than those which prevail at present. There is a fashion in opprobrium as in other things, and it appears to be fashionable to reproach these voluntary institutions with the small percentage of their good cases, and to question their efficiency and expediency. Even if their visible success were far less than it is, the Labour Colonies and Depots established by philanthropic agencies are deserving of the highest praise. They are trying to discharge, with inadequate resources, and with little public recognition, the duty of society towards two large classes of people—the unemployed and the unemployable, and they would have work enough of the same kind to do, even were Detention Institutions of the kind proposed in full operation.

The existing Labour Colonies and Depots would be specially useful in dealing with men who were temporarily unemployable owing to physical and moral deterioration. The Detention Colonies could not be expected to yield satisfactory results if they were handicapped with inmates of this kind, who belong rather to infirmaries than to workshops. Hence, in committing a physical wreck, incapable of immediate employment, the magistrates should have discretion to order the first part of his sentence to be passed in one of these Voluntary Institutions, where he would be able to receive more particular, and perhaps more sympathetic, treatment than would be possible in a hard-working Labour House. If, in the opinion of the authorities, the effect of this recuperative treatment made it unnecessary to pass the man, when fit, into a Detention Colony, there to complete his sentence, he would be released on parole, on the understanding that he would be liable to immediate reapprehension if his conduct gave rise to complaint. The Voluntary Colonies would continue to be managed as at present, but they would be entitled to grants of public money, the amount of which should be dependent less upon the exact number of cases received from the magistrates, than upon the rescue work of all kinds in which they were engaged, for this work is one of common advantage, and it is indefensible that the whole burden of cost should be borne by voluntary well-wishers.

Before leaving the question of repressive measures, it can hardly be superfluous to say that much could be done at once to discourage vagrancy and loafing if greater discrimination in almsgiving were shown. It sounds paradoxical, but it is true, that many of the people who, by their thoughtless doles, make loafers, are among the warmest friends of institutions called into existence for the one purpose of unmaking them. Nothing in the world is easier than to get rid of an importunate beggar by the gift of a coin; nothing is more difficult than to undo the harm which results, in most cases, from this open incitement to a life of idleness. To the average man all benevolence of this kind is a virtue; Emerson knew better when he spoke of the "vicious shillings" which he gave indiscriminately and against his better judgment. In Tudor times attempts were made by law to check almsgiving, insofar as it encouraged idleness and vagrancy;[50] and as late as 1744 (17 George II.) a law was passed exposing to a penalty of not less than 10s. or more than 40s. (or in default, one month's detention in a house of correction), any person who knowingly gave to a rogue or vagabond lodging or shelter and refrained from handing him over to a constable. Legislation of this kind is still in operation on the Continent. In 1889 the Canon of Schwyz, in democratic Switzerland, passed a law making "persons, who, by giving alms, favour begging from house to house or in the street," liable to a fine of 10 francs. Some time ago, also, a police ordinance was issued in the Uelzen district of Prussia, to the following effect:—

"(1) The giving of alms of any kind whatever to mendicant vagrants is prohibited on pain of a fine not exceeding 9 marks (9s.).

"(2) The giving of food and clothing for the relief of visible want is as before subject to no penalty, provided that there be no possibility of the recipient exchanging such gifts for money or brandy."

The legal prohibition in this country of indiscriminate charity, so called, even when offered to mendicants, and thus contributing to illegality, would nowadays be regarded as so serious an invasion of the "liberty of the subject" as to be inconceivable, and no writer who has a due reverence for that august principle would propose it.[51] Much may be done to discourage the practice, however, by educating public opinion to a recognition of the fact that only the philanthropy that is wise and well-directed can be truly helpful and beneficent.

The further question follows: What part, then, might the existing workhouse continue to play in our Poor Law system? In my opinion a part far more important than it has played in the past. For when the tramp and the loafer have been disposed of, there will remain the dependent and infirm poor, to the relief of whose needs it might, under improved conditions, be henceforth exclusively and more intelligently devoted. As, however, it would be no longer a workhouse, even to the extent of its casual wards, it would be expedient from every standpoint to discard for ever the hard name which it now bears, and to return to the earlier and less repulsive name of Poorhouse. One need not be very old to be able to recall the time when the name Bastille ("Basty," with a long "y," was the popular distortion of the word in my native

Yorkshire), was the name by which the poorer classes universally expressed their horror of the workhouse: so much of modern French history had reached their contracted minds. That ill-repute has to some extent been outlived, yet the evil that institutions, as well as men, do lives after them, and an intense prejudice against the workhouse is still laudably common amongst the more deserving poor, and it will persist so long as the present name lasts, in spite of all that may be done to humanise our principles and methods of Poor Law administration. Poorhouses, of some sort, however named, we shall need to have so long as a Poor Law is necessary; and when the stigma has been removed from honest poverty, there is no reason to believe that the deserving recipients of public relief would show the old sense of humiliation and dread when necessity decrees their passage through portals which would no longer be those of hopeless indignity but of honourable comfort.

Happily, the improvement of these institutions proceeds apace, and to my mind the best thing is to continue improving them until they are good enough to serve as asylums for the most deserving of our aged and infirm poor, and infinitely too good for the idle and worthless. Several years ago the writer of the annual "Legal Poor of London" article in *The Times* called attention to the ameliorative influences which are so actively working in the metropolitan workhouses, and questioned whether too much was not being done for the inmates of these places:—

> "For aged and deserving inmates," he said, "discipline is relaxed, the wards are made comfortable with carpets, window curtains, table covers, and arm chairs, and the cheery day rooms are supplied with literature, while a certain amount of privacy is allowed. The dietary has been improved, the electric light established, and warmth and comfort prevail, the inmates having no care as to the provision of maintenance. It is not surprising that they 'appear to appreciate' such attentions, nor is it matter for wonder that additions are made to their numbers. Nobody desires to see the poor, especially the aged poor, who are compelled to resort to the workhouse, treated otherwise than in a humane way; but sound views should prevail; and if we are to reckon the piling up of comforts in the workhouses as being 'so much to the good in the organisation of the life of the otherwise destitute poor,' we must be prepared to see thousands of ratepayers who are now less eligibly placed than the inmates of the workhouse, and whose burdens, in having to contribute to the maintenance of those inmates in greater comfort than themselves, are annually growing heavier, added to our

present mass of indoor pauperism. Old age pauperism, encouraged by the altered conditions of the workhouses, has really become a serious question."

That is one aspect of the question, but there is another. The really pertinent point is, are the conditions of life nowadays prevalent in the workhouse in themselves too humane; do they go beyond the requirements of our modern civilisation? If not, there is no justification for holding the reforming hand. The right thing, surely, is to level up the conditions of life outside. Just as the admirable example set by so many public authorities in the treatment of their servants exerts a favourable influence in favour of employees in private service, so the standard of life insisted upon for the public workhouse, infirmary and asylum is bound to react upon the homes and habits of the independent labouring classes. If the workman who is taxed to keep the pauper in tolerable comfort does not enjoy at least equal conditions of existence himself, he will ask himself, and then others, the reason why. And who will blame him for so doing? Least of all the sociologist, who knows that no factor in the civilisation of society is more potent or more irresistible than the expansion of one's view of life and the multiplication of rational needs.

There remain the *bona-fide* seekers of work. For them no adequate provision exists, and the neglect to make it is a crying wrong. The present indiscriminate treatment of all wayfarers works unjustly in every way. It is unfair to the dissolute idler, whom it confirms in his sloth; it is monstrously unfair to the unwilling idler, whom it penalises for his misfortune. When society has done its duty to the tramp, it will not hesitate to recognise its responsibilities towards the genuine unemployed. It will do so not from motives of philanthropy alone, though it is a platitude to say that a society which professes to be based on Christian principles owes far more than it has ever paid or acknowledged to its workless members; it will do it also from considerations of social interest and well-being, recognising that it is the best charity and the truest economy to get an idle man's hands employed as soon as possible, the worst extravagance to allow him to remain unproductive a day longer than can be avoided. Labour is the first element in all wealth-creation, and every idle man is, in greater or less degree, a source of national impoverishment, for he is consuming without producing.

Wherever public labour registries have been established as part of a co-ordinated system, as in Bavaria and other parts of Germany, and in Switzerland, it has been found that, short of a free use of the railway, which is no doubt the ideal arrangement, hostels for decent wayfarers of the working class are essential. Those who think that such institutions are superfluous will do well to read the following story told by a working man correspondent in *The Times*:—

"Last summer some two hundred of us were given a week's notice, through slackness of work, by a powerful London company, and, although we all brought characters when we entered the company's service, we were informed on discharge that the company never gave references, and would not answer any letters with regard to our characters. Now, as everyone in London requires a personal character, unless we have influence at our back what chance have we for anything but casual work? One of the men, in despair of finding employment in London, left for the Lincolnshire potato harvest. He tells me that, not having money for all his journey, he walked down, and on several occasions had to put up at a casual ward, where he had to break 13 cwt. of stones in return for the shelter from the rain for the night. He says in some unions one has to lay on boards, with filthy rugs for bedclothes, and only dry bread to eat at meals, except at dinner, when you are allowed 1½ oz. of cheese. To avoid this organised charity he one night crept into a cart-shed. He was there found by the police, and by the goodness of the magistrates was sent on by train to Lincoln, and at the expense of the country provided with free board and lodge for fourteen days at the prison there. On being released he was fortunate enough to obtain work in the harvest fields, and being an all round good worker followed up a threshing machine all the winter till now. This is only one case, due entirely to the fact that many large firms will not give characters to men on discharge."

The incidents here recorded afford a striking illustration of a passage in the report of the Lindsey Quarter Sessions Committee on Vagrancy:—

"With regard to the man seeking work, your Committee are of opinion that the present methods of dealing with vagrancy constitute a real danger.... A certain number of such men find their way into our prisons owing to their failure to establish their *bona fide* character as working men before the courts. The temptation afterward to drift gradually into the ranks of the professional tramp class is considerable. Loss of manual or technical skill soon follows, and the man who ought to be a producer becomes a costly burden to the community."

To distinguish between the genuine work-seeker and the fraud would be no difficult task. All that would be necessary would be to require the former to authenticate himself by a way-ticket or pass, attested either by the police, a trade union, a labour bureau, or a recent responsible employer.[52] On the strength of such a certificate, which a *bona-fide* applicant should have a right to demand, unless good reasons existed to the contrary, he might well be allowed to proceed on his journey, and be admitted to such public hostels as happened to lie in his way. Vagabondage pure and simple would be a game no longer worth the candle. If the itinerant were an industrial malingerer, the fact would speedily come to light, and with no Poor Law to fall back upon, the sure prospect of detention in a Labour House would await him. The entire supplanting of the so-called "model" lodging-houses by travellers' hostels in public hands would be one of the greatest benefits that could be conferred upon the working classes.

It is worthy of note that the use of way-tickets, minus the houses of call now proposed, is not unknown to English legislation on vagrancy. So long ago as 1824 an Act was passed empowering magistrates to grant certificates or passes to vagrants discharged from prison, to enable them to reach their places of settlement, and to obtain relief from parochial authorities on the way, though this pass system appears to have been carried out in four counties only, and to have soon fallen into disuse. Further, a Minute of the old Poor Law Board, dated August 4, 1848, in recommending differential treatment as between the work-seeking and the work-shy wayfarer, urged, in particular, that the former should be helped by a system of way-tickets, applicable to fixed routes and valid for a definite period.

> "There is obviously a wide distinction," said the Minute, " between those who are temporarily and unavoidably in distress and the habitual tramp or vagrant who simulates destitution; and one of the worst results of the present undiscriminating treatment of all who are commonly denominated 'casuals' is, that some of the most fitting objects of public charity are subjected to the discomforts that were intended to repel the worthless. Among all the unfortunate there are none whose destitution is more unquestionable, and whose hard lot presents stronger claims to sympathy, than the widow and orphan, deprived, at a distance from home, of their natural supporter, and the honest artisan or labourer who is seeking the employment of which accidental circumstances have suddenly deprived him. Yet, under the present system, such persons as these either share the discomforts, the filth, the turbulence, and the demoralising fellowship of the thief, the mendicant and the prostitute, who crowd the vagrant wards of the workhouses, or are compelled to brave the inclemency of

the weather and the pains of hunger by reason of their unconquerable aversion to such companionship.

"It would not appear to be difficult to establish a system by which this deserving class of persons might be furnished with such evidence of their character and circumstances as might afford a fair presumption of the truth of their plea of destitution. A wayfarer of this class might, at the place where the cause of destitution occurs, be enabled by those who are cognisant of it to obtain a certificate from some proper authority, setting forth his name, the cause of destitution, and the object and destination of his journey. On his presenting this certificate at any workhouse, the master, on finding that it was satisfactory, that the applicant was on the road to his destination, and that he was without money or other means, might at once admit him, and supply him with the usual accommodation of the inmates. In this way the honest but destitute wayfarer, possessed of such credentials, would obtain the advantage of being admitted into the workhouse without reference to the relieving officer, and also of receiving better accommodation, than that at present afforded to him in the vagrant ward."

The plan proposed appears to have been followed but little. It was reported to the Poor Law Board in 1865 that it was in force in one county only (Essex), where vagrancy had been practically abolished as a result.

It is more to the purpose to know that, at the present time, way-tickets in a modified form are in use in some of the southern counties of England—Sussex, Wiltshire, Gloucestershire, Berkshire—and in parts of Wales. The best known system is that of Berkshire, which was adopted in Gloucestershire and Wiltshire in 1882, and is still in efficient operation. Its object is to enable a work-seeker to move through the county to his destination by the most direct route, and without unnecessary delay, and by providing him with lodging, supper, and breakfast at the casual ward, and with a mid-day meal on his going, to remove all necessity for begging from the public. The system was thus described to the Vagrancy Committee by Lieut. Col. J. Curtis Hayward, Chairman of the Gloucestershire Poor Law Vagrancy Committee:—

"A vagrant on entering the county gets a ticket from the assistant relieving officer who, in most cases, in our county is a police officer. That ticket has marked upon it his final destination and his description. With that he goes to the casual ward, where, of course, he is dealt with in the ordinary way; he gets his food night and morning and he has to do his task. When he leaves, the master puts on the ticket the name of the union which he has to go to next day—it must be on the road to his final destination—and also the name of a bread station. We have got one in nearly every case half-way. Sometimes he has to go a little out of his way to a bread station. It is also a police station. If he arrives there between one and three, he is given a ticket on a baker close by.

"If he arrives at the union entered upon the ticket that evening, he has what we call a good ticket; if, on the other hand, he arrives at some other union, or has no ticket at all, he is given a new one and it is considered a bad ticket. Our committee recommend the boards of guardians to detain, for one night only, all those who show they are passing as quickly as they can to the destination which they say they are going to; and to detain for two nights all those without any tickets, or who show that they are not going straight to their destination.

"For instance, supposing a man says, 'I am going from Gloucester to Cardiff,' he would have, perhaps, 'Westbury' marked on his ticket to go to; and suppose he turned up at Stroud, which is directly in the opposite direction, we would say:—'That is not where you are going to; this is a bad ticket; you must have a new ticket, and you will be detained two nights.'

"We give everybody a ticket. That is different to what they have done in Worcestershire and other places, where they do not give a ticket. They tried to discriminate between ... the *bona-fide* working men and those who were not *bona-fide*. We never attempt to make any distinction, because we say giving this ticket is taking away the excuse for begging; therefore, we say every man ought to have a ticket in his pocket."

The system in force in Wiltshire was described to the same Committee by Mr. A. C. Mitchell, Chairman of the Poor Law Vagrancy Committee of that county:—

"The system was shortly this—that on a tramp applying at the first union he arrived at in the county for relief, he was given a way-ticket on which was entered his description, his final destination, and the places where he would call.

Arrangements were made at convenient places where a police constable was stationed, where the tramp could get bread between workhouses which necessitated a fair day's march. This ticket, as long as he proceeded in the direction to the final destination to which he declared himself to be proceeding, entitled him to eight ounces of bread (in Gloucestershire it was a larger amount at first, now it is eight ounces), between the hours of twelve and two at the given stations. As long as he kept on his way to his final destination that held good between union and union.

"The man is passed on from point to point, as long as he keeps on the route originally described, and he obtains his meals of bread at a given point in the middle of each day, between the hours of twelve and two.

"If that man varies his route, according to the recommendations of our committee—of course we cannot be responsible for the actions of boards of guardians—he would then be in the same position as the man who arrived without a ticket at all, and would be liable to full detention under the Casual Poor Act, 1882.

"We advise the boards of guardians that if a man has his ticket in order, he shall be forwarded on his road at the earliest possible time, after having broken the portion of stones for his one night's detention."

The same system is in operation in West and East Sussex, and as late as 1908 the Poor Law Inspector for those districts reported to the Local Government Board:—

"As regards vagrancy, the way-ticket system in operation in West Sussex is reported to be working well, and is looked upon as a permanent institution. It has also been extended to East Sussex. A considerable reduction took place in the number of vagrants relieved in Kent and Sussex."[53]

In the following chapters the measures which have been adopted in Continental countries for dealing with the social parasite will be considered in detail.

CHAPTER IV.

THE BELGIAN BEGGARS' DEPOTS.

The legislation of Belgium for the treatment of vagrants and mendicants experimented in many directions before it established forced Labour Houses and Colonies for the detention of these offenders. As early as 1793, during the Dutch connection, a Decree (October 15) was issued, making vagrancy and mendicancy misdemeanours punishable by detention in a house of correction for one year, while vagrants on a second conviction, and beggars on a third, were liable to transportation. A law of July 5, 1808, again formally prohibited begging, and provided for the detention of offenders in forced Labour Houses; and the Penal Code of October 12, 1810, awarded imprisonment, followed by Labour House detention, to loafers generally. The last-named law does not appear to have been stringently enforced, and it was relaxed in 1848, in consequence of which act vagrancy and begging increased. The result was a new law of March 6, 1866, imposing heavier penalties on able-bodied loafers of all kinds, though vagrancy was punished more severely than simple mendicancy. By reason of this law some of the old Labour Houses were abolished, and a large central institution was established at Merxplas, in the Province of Flanders, for the detention of all classes of offenders for disciplinary treatment. A little later the penalties for vagrancy and begging were reduced, and a more radical amendment of the law took place in 1891, the effect of which was to take away from these offences a penal character.

Under this law, the beggar, the tramp, and the loafer are dealt with at the present time. The great difference between the original Belgian Labour Houses and the Beggars' Depots of to-day lies in the fact that the earlier institutions were managed by philanthropic associations, while those existing to-day are State establishments, and form part of the judicial system of the country.

The law of November 27, 1891[54] (which came into force on January 4, 1892), for the repression of vagrancy and mendicity required the Government to organise correctional institutions of three kinds, *viz*.: (*a*) Beggars' Depots (*dépôts de mendicité*); (*b*) Houses of Refuge (*maisons de refuge*), and Reformatory Schools (*écoles de bienfaisance*). The institutions of the first two kinds are commonly spoken of as Labour Houses or Colonies in Belgium. There are two Beggars' Depots, the central one for men at Merxplas, near Antwerp, and a small one for women at Bruges; and there are three Houses of Refuge, *viz*., Wortel and Hoogstraeten (managed as one establishment) for men, and one at Bruges for women.

The law states that the Beggars' Depots shall be "exclusively devoted to the confinement of persons whom the Judicial Authority shall place at the disposal of the Government" for that purpose. Such persons are of the following classes: (*a*) Able-bodied persons who, instead of working for their living, depend upon charity as professional beggars; (*b*) persons who, owing to idleness, drunkenness, or immorality, live in a state of vagrancy; and (*c*) *souteneurs*. These persons may be committed by the magistrates for a period not less than two nor more than seven years. Moreover, vagrants and beggars who have been sentenced by a Correctional Court to imprisonment for less than a year, may be ordered to undergo detention in a Depot at the end of the sentence for not less than one year or more than seven years, just as offenders of the same kind are sent to Labour Houses in Germany and Austria after undergoing imprisonment. It is provided, however, that the Minister of Justice may, at any time, order the release of persons confined in a Depot, should he be of opinion that their further confinement is unnecessary. In order to give the loafer a chance of voluntary reformation, he is on a first conviction sent to a House of Refuge by way of probation for a period not exceeding one year, or until he shall have earned 12s. On re-conviction, his certain destination is the Depot of Merxplas, with its severer discipline. The House of Refuge is provided for the reception of (*a*) persons handed over by a Judicial Authority to the Government for simple detention, and (*b*) persons whose restraint may be asked for by a Communal Authority, though those of the latter class must enter of their own free will if over eighteen years of age. In general, the House of Refuge is intended for vagrants, mendicants, loafers, and dissolute persons who are not thought to deserve the treatment of incorrigible offenders. The voluntary inmates correspond very closely to the typical unemployed person who applies for task work in our English workhouses. In no case may detention exceed a year, unless with the detainee's acquiescence, and as in the case of the Beggars' Depots, the Minister of Justice may order the immediate discharge of any person whose further confinement may appear to him unnecessary.

In the institutions of both types small daily wages are paid, except when withdrawn as a measure of discipline, and a portion of every man's earnings is put away as a leaving fund (*masse de sortie*), to be paid out to him in cash, clothing and tools. In no case is a well behaving colonist allowed to leave penniless. A minimum sum of 4s. is given to every such man, whether he has earned it or not; those guilty of misconduct or idleness take away their savings, however small, and no more. The Minister of Justice approves the scale of payment for every class of work in the two institutions.

The cost of maintenance of persons sent by a judicial authority to the Depot or House of Refuge is borne, in equal shares, by the State, the Provinces, and the Communes in which the persons have their settlement, but infirm persons are maintained altogether by their settlement communes, which likewise bear the whole cost in the case of persons detained in a House of Refuge at their own request. Where a person, detained by judicial decision, has no settlement, the costs of maintenance fall on the province in which he was arrested or brought before the Court; in the case of *souteneurs* the cost is borne by the Communes in which they pursued their practices. Costs of maintenance can, however, be recovered from the persons concerned, or those legally liable for their support.

The following were the admissions in the Beggars' Depots and the Houses of Refuge for the first fifteen years after the Act came into force:—

ADMISSIONS TO BEGGARS' DEPOTS.

Year.	Number of Admissions.			Mean Number of Inmates.
	Male.	Female.	Total.	
1892	6,147	666	6,813	3,564
1893	3,482	352	3,834	4,324
1894	4,141	393	4,534	4,193
1895	3,722	333	4,055	4,592
1896	3,224	292	3,516	4,430
1897	3,115	266	3,381	4,076
1898	3,339	284	3,623	4,208
1899	3,018	215	3,233	4,248
1900	3,547	253	3,800	4,058
1901	4,348	275	4,623	4,542
1902	4,514	252	4,776	4,865
1903	4,649	386	5,035	5,054
1904	4,615	275	4,890	5,132
1905	4,624	260	4,884	5,450
1906	4,246	268	4,694	5,351

ADMISSIONS TO HOUSES OF REFUGE.

Year.	Number of Admissions.			Mean Number of Inmates.
	Male.	Female.	Total.	
1892	6,139	775	6,914	2,043
1893	4,411	942	5,353	2,145
1894	4,593	519	5,112	2,902
1895	4,559	414	4,973	2,766
1896	3,805	360	4,165	2,314
1897	3,745	323	4,068	1,876
1898	3,770	343	4,113	1,983
1899	3,398	258	3,656	1,823
1900	3,586	266	3,852	1,691
1901	4,174	261	4,435	1,761
1902	4,389	252	4,614	1,876
1903	3,428	278	3,706	1,733
1904	3,546	221	3,767	1,620
1905	3,057	194	3,252	1,352
1904	2,505	184	2,289	1,176

The Labour Colony of Merxplas is unique as a centralised State reformatory for loafers, and, owing to its large extent, the excellence of its arrangements, and not least, the rational principles upon which it is administered, it fully deserves the study and the praise which have been bestowed upon it by foreign observers. On the whole, it would seem to correspond more nearly than any other Continental institution for forced labour to the special needs of this country.

The buildings of Merxplas are grouped together in convenient positions, and are of a very substantial kind. The principal blocks contain the offices, the several classes of dormitories, the workshops, the stores, the exercise wings, the dining hall, the church, the hospital, the prison, and the barracks, for a small guard of 150 men is stationed on the premises for cases of emergency. Well-made roads intersect the grounds in various directions, and there is a large amount of open space.

The inmates of Merxplas are divided into six classes: (1) Men sentenced for offences against morality and for arson; (2) men sentenced to Colony life as a sequel to a term of imprisonment of less than one year, and men whose past history shows them to be dangerous to the community; (3) habitual vagabonds, mendicants, inebriates, and men generally unable to support themselves; (4) men under twenty-one years of age; (5) infirm and incurable persons; and (6) first offenders. In December, 1907, the inmates were divided amongst these classes in the following proportions: (1) 169; (2) 328; (3) 3,033; (4) 20; (5) 1,425; (6) 40; total, 5,015.

The men in Classes (1) and (2) are detained in special quarters, and under special supervision, and work apart from the rest, with whom they have no intercourse whatever, being, in fact, treated as criminals. The only difference between Classes (3) and (4) in regard to treatment is that the younger men are kept separate from the older, and that a portion of their time is devoted to school. The infirm in Class (5) are able to do light work, while the incurables do none. Class (6) explains itself. All the offenders, except those in Class (5), are allowed to earn wages on the scale applying to their employment; those in Class (6) are given canteen money of 3 centimes per day for the purchase of small luxuries. As has been explained, the minimum sentence of detention is two years, but owing to the exercise of the Minister's prerogative of pardon, the average term of confinement is about sixteen months.

The small staff of eighty warders (with the military guard to fall back upon), under a chief director and two deputy directors, is found sufficient to control the movements of this great army of "irregulars"; in addition, there are one doctor, two priests, five teachers, nineteen clerks, one manufacturing manager, and six sisters of mercy. Many reliable men are, however, chosen from the ranks of the prisoners to assist in the superintendence of work.

The offenders dealt with during the seven years 1902 to 1908 were as follows:—

MERXPLAS BEGGARS' DEPOT (MEN).

	1902	1903	1904	1905	1906	1907	1908
Admitted	4,514	4,649	4,615	4,624	4,426	4,212	4,431
Discharged	2,847	2,922	2,827	2,666	2,935	2,792	2,282
Transferred	501	452	514	439	504	464	478
Absconded	879	1,004	1,066	1,243	1,031	919	1,055
Died	125	108	112	94	136	134	139

Total	4,352	4,486	4,519	4,442	4,606	4,309	3,954
Detained on December 31	4,851	5,014	5,110	5,292	5,112	5,015	5,492

The admissions shown above included the reinstatements (of inmates escaped) after capture, and the admissions by transfer from other institutions. The direct admissions, the admissions by transfer, and the reinstatements after escape are here shown separately for the years 1901 to 1908:—

	1901	1902	1903	1904	1905	1906
Admitted direct	3,280	3,390	3,460	3,316	3,186	3,071
Discharged owing to expiration of sentence and Ministerial decision, conducted to the frontier, and deceased	2,436	2,972	3,030	2,939	2,760	3,071
Admitted by transfer	391	353	305	366	341	431
Discharged by transfer	530	501	452	514	439	504
Reinstated after escape	677	771	884	933	1,097	924
Escaped	769	879	1,004	1,066	1,243	1,031

Those "placed at the disposition of the Government" (for commitment to the Merxplas Depot) under the law of November 27, 1891, during the years 1901 to 1906 belonged to the following classes:—

	1901	1902	1903	1904	1905	1906
Able-bodied beggars and vagrants (Article 13)	4,314	4,509	4,637	4,614	4,618	4,419
Able-bodied beggars and vagrants for detention	14	5	12	1	6	7

supplementary to imprisonment (Article 14)	4,348	4,514	4,649	4,615	4,624	4,426
Deduct reinstatements after escape	677	771	884	933	1,097	924

The following further table shows the frequency of commitment during a series of years:—

Number of Times Committed.	1902	1903	1904	1905	1906	1907	1908
For the first time	674	668	558	517	547	519	720
For the second time	546	585	552	595	522	442	561
For the third time	493	472	582	516	488	433	465
For the fourth time	446	470	455	406	420	406	425
For the fifth time or oftener	2,355	2,454	2,468	2,590	2,449	2,412	2,260
Total number of admissions	4,514	4,649	4,615	4,624	4,426	4,212	4,431

The whole of the men capable of working, either much or little, are employed according to their aptitudes and physical capacity, either in farm and land work, in the workshops, in domestic work in and around the establishment, or in the service of outside employers. On a given day in 1907, 1,279 men were engaged on the farm and land, 1,970 in industrial work for the profit of the Colony, 811 in domestic work, and 525 were lent to other institutions.

The men engaged in the fields work in gangs of between fifty and sixty, each under a single overseer. Shelters exist for their accommodation in wet weather, and when it is impossible to do outside work they are employed in the workshops.

The trades and occupations are very numerous, but the principal are brick, pipe and tile making, iron founding, button making, wood-working, mat, boot, and shoe making, weaving, tanning, tailoring, carpentering, and printing.

Several years ago, a Committee appointed by the Lindsey (Lincoln) Quarter Sessions visited Merxplas and reported as follows upon what they saw of the workshops:—[55]

> "Each shop was under a trade instructor. The men appeared to be working cheerfully and diligently. As wages were higher in the shops, we were told that it was made a privilege to work there. All the shops were large and airy, and the following were the principal industries being carried on at the time of our visit.
>
> "In the ironfoundry they were making their own patterns, doing their own casting, turning, and finishing for everything in the way of metal used in the establishment, from cast iron window frames to brass pumps.
>
> "Next to this was a very large shop for making cement tiles, working for outside firms on a recently invented system of employing hydraulic cement and colours to furnish tiles of elaborate colouring and patterns. This shop was on a large scale, and doing remunerative work, and impressed us very much.
>
> "The mat making shop was of the ordinary kind, but on a very large scale. Every description of mat, from the sennet to the thick pile mat worked in patterns, was made.
>
> "The weaving shop presented an interesting industry, which could be easily learned by the unskilled, namely that of making yarn of cowhair, which is afterwards worked into carpets. Other men were busy spinning the thread for the warp of the cloth used for the colonists' clothes. A large portion of this shop was also occupied by hand-looms in full work, where the cloth itself was being woven.
>
> "The button shop, for making mother of pearl buttons for the outside trade, has been newly started. This shop formed an exception, in that all the lathes were bought from outside, none being made at Merxplas.
>
> "In the carpenters' shop was a prison van which was made entirely by colonist labour, with the one exception of the springs. There was an order on hand for 1,100 window frames for a new prison. We also saw there some excellent

furniture, large numbers of chairs, travelling trunks, and cabinet work of all kinds.

"The cobblers were busy on boots for the Army, which were hand-made throughout. Here they were also making hospital shoes from the selvage of cloth woven on a block; a very ingenious method of utilising waste material.

"All the printing required for the colonies is also done in a printing shop.

"In another small shop about twenty men were employed in making fine chains for sham jewellery.

"The brick works were large, employing thirty-six men at brick-making, exclusive of those employed at the furnaces, and the clay-getters. The usual number of bricks made was about 70,000 daily, the men being paid 15 centimes (1·4*d*.) per 1,000.

"On an equally large scale was the making of cement conduit pipes. The cement is made at a factory in the neighbourhood, and the white sand is also bought.

"After visiting the brickworks we passed through small shops of stone-masons and sculptors to the pottery and the tannery. The last had a large number of hides in preparation, and uses bark from the trees of the estate, but not exclusively.

"To the north of the workshops the three-winged building is a store. Here we saw a quantity of bar iron, one of the few materials that Merxplas cannot itself produce.

"Here was also the clothing store. The cloth is made throughout by the colonists, with the one exception of the 'fulling' process, which requires special machinery. The material was of several different kinds, including two varieties for officers' uniform, and all that is required for the winter and summer clothing of the colonists. Civilian clothes and tools, also made in the colony, can be purchased by the colonists when they are liberated. In the centre were several large rooms full of the private clothes and other belongings of the colonists, each in their own bag, and all remarkably free from any offensive odour.

"The farming seemed to be carried on on the same excellent principles as the workshops. The crops of maize and hemp were remarkably tall (the latter supplies the raw material for rope making), and the fields generally seemed thoroughly worked and tilled. The cowhouse and piggeries were very clean, and all the buildings were of excellent design and well-built. A large number of horses and oxen are kept for farm work, as not much spade cultivation is used. There is a large herd of milking cows to supply the hospital, and a considerable number of young stock and sheep are also kept, the latter being housed and hand-fed in winter. The whole of the products are consumed in the colony, and, as is the practice in the shops, very little machinery is used, whilst a large amount of labour is employed in bringing fresh ground under cultivation. The sandy top-soil is first removed and immense quantities of Antwerp street sweepings and clay rubbish are put on. Large gangs are also employed in hand-weeding, and all the advantages of farming with abundance of cheap labour are conspicuous."

The accounts of a recent year show proceeds of trades as follows: Mat making, £4,200; weaving, £5,753; shoe making, £1,324; brick paving, £1,266; forge and foundry, £1,847; tobacco, £1,671; tanning, £1,852; tailoring, £3,600; furniture, £1,346, and brick making, £1,913. The profits on twenty-six trades in 1907 were said to be £4,072.

The usual work-day consists of about ten hours in summer, and between seven and nine in winter, broken by three intervals for meals and rest. The day's routine is as follows:—

SUMMER

Week-days.	April 1 to September 15.	September 16 to October 31.
Rise	4.30 a.m.	5.0 a.m.
Distribution of bread	5.0 "	5.30 "
Work	5.45 "	6.15 "
Doctor's visit	7.0 "	7.0 "
First meal and rest	8.0 "	8.0 "
Work	8.30 "	8.30 "

Director's report	8.30	"	8.30	"
Director's report	10.0	"	10.0	"
Second meal—in two parties	10.40 11.40	"	10.40 11.40	"
Work	1.15	p.m.	1.15	p.m.
Rest	4.0	"	4.0	"
Work	4.30	"	4.30	"
Third meal	6.45	"	6.45	"
Bed	7.0	"	7.0	"
Sunday.				
General medical inspection	After mass.		After mass.	
Mass	7.0 and 8.0 a.m.		7.0 and 8.0 a.m.	
Vespers	2.30	p.m.	2.30	p.m.

WINTER

Week-days.	April 1 to November 1 to February 15.		February 16 to March 31	
Rise	6.0	a.m.	5.30	a.m.
Distribution of bread and coffee	6.30	"	6.00	"
Work	7.15	"	6.45	"
Doctor's visit	8.0	"	8.0	"
Director's report	10.0	"	10.0	"
Second meal—in two parties	10.40 11.40	"	10.40 11.40	"
Work	1.15	p.m.	1.15	p.m.
Third meal	4.0	"	5.0	"

Bed	4.30	"	5.30	"
Sunday.				
General medical inspection	After mass.		After mass.	
Mass	8.0 and 9.0 a.m.		8.0 and 9.0 a.m.	
Vespers	2.0 p.m.		2.0 p.m.	
Sunday.				
General medical inspection	After mass.	After mass.		
Mass	8.0 and 9.0 a.m.	8.0 and 9.0 a.m.		
Vespers	2.0 p.m.	2.0 p.m.		

It may be noted that the diet of the colonists, while varied, is almost exclusively vegetarian, but the inmates may supplement their ordinary food by extras purchasable at the canteen at cost price.

There is no doubt that great organising ability is shown in the industrial management of Merxplas. The ruling principles are the following:—

(1) Machinery is used as little as possible. The lathes in the workshops are driven by hand-power. The weaving is done by hand looms. Even the grinding is done by a large capstan wheel worked by two relays of sixty men each.

(2) The raw material is, as far as possible, produced in the Colony. Tobacco, flax, and chicory are grown on the farm; the leather comes from the farm cattle, and is tanned on the spot by bark obtained from the woods; and the hair of the same cattle is spun by the inmates for carpet making.

(3) Every effort is directed towards making the Colony self-contained. As far as possible, the buildings, with their fittings and furniture, are done by the colonists. The lathes and tools are made from raw metal. The boots and shoes, cloth, tobacco, and a multitude of other articles are from first to last produced on the spot.

The earnings of the inmates depend upon the character of the work done. The existing scale for able-bodied men, as sanctioned by the Minister of Justice in 1903, is as follows (10½ centimes = 1d.):—

	Centimes Per Day.
Industrial work	15 to 25
Farm work	12 to 21
Domestic, garden, and other work	12 to 18
Offices of trust (writers, porters, hospital and store assistants, shepherds, dairy and stablemen, butchers, etc.)	20 to 30
Punishment and disciplinary sections	10 to 15

The rule is to pay the inmates, at first, the minimum rates which apply to their class of work. Small bonuses and gratuities are given in special cases. Extra duties, such as reading aloud fiction in the dormitories (to prevent conversation), singing in church, and service in the bugle squad, are paid for. Non-able-bodied men receive "canteen money" of 3 centimes per day.

The men are paid monthly one half of their earnings to spend as they wish, and the balance goes to their leaving fund, and is paid only on discharge. As a rule, the instalments paid go in the purchase of supplementary food and luxuries, but many frugal workers deposit the whole of their earnings in the leaving fund. The result is that some men, who have been detained a long time, have been known to take away as much as £8 in cash, clothes, and tools.

The Colony's chief sources of revenue are; (1) The maintenance charges of 66 centimes (6½d.) per head per day for able-bodied colonists, and 1 franc 50 centimes (1s. 3d.) for non-able-bodied colonists needing special food, paid in equal shares by the State, the Provinces, and the Communes; (2) the proceeds of the colonists' labour, both on the farm and in the workshops; and (3) the profits of the canteen.

An estimate of revenue and expenditure for the year 1905, prepared by the Director of Merxplas for the Departmental Vagrancy Committee, contained the following principal items:—

Revenue.

	£
Maintenance grants (3,500 able-bodied inmates at 66 centimes per day, and 1,000 not able-bodied inmates at 1 franc 50 centimes per day) sheep, pigs, etc.) to private persons	55,626
Sale of farm produce (milk, vegetables, butter,	800
Produce of workshops (sold to private persons, prisons, charitable institutions, and discharged inmates)	15,000
Canteen	3,800
Miscellaneous	399
Total	£75,625

Expenditure.

	£
Salaries and allowances, permanent staff, etc.	9,329
Office, library, and school	220
Buildings and furniture	2,400
Maintenance and clothing	23,254
Colonists' earnings	11,720
Canteen (goods purchased)	1,960
Workshops (tools, raw materials, etc.)	14,181
Farm and estate (plants, seeds, manures, live stock, straw and fodder, etc.)	2,047
Miscellaneous	1,020
Total	£66,131

It will be seen that a credit balance of £9,494 is shown, but this is obviously a paper balance, inasmuch as no allowance is made for rent, interest on capital, or depreciation. On the other hand, in any full balance sheet a large accretion of capital value through improvements would be shown.

On this subject Monsieur Stroobant writes to me:—

> "The property of Merxplas belongs to the State, and its value increases every year because of the new buildings erected, the plantations, and the improvements made to the land. In 1870, there were only several small farms, heath and fir woods. The land had an area of about 650 hectares, and as the land was poor, its value was probably £12 per hectare."[56] The present value has never been accurately appraised, but I place it at £200,000. The increased value of the estate has been produced entirely by the labour of the detainees, Parliament having made no further grant for new buildings. The whole of the buildings were progressively erected between 1870 and 1895, according to the resources at disposal, but after a fixed plan conceived in a large spirit by the architect, Monsieur Besme."

Taking the accounts as published, the cost of the inmates during the years 1901 to 1906 was as follows:—

	1901.	1902.	1903.	1904.	1905.	1906.
Number of able-bodied detainees	3,702	3,799	3,842	3,716	3,645	3,440
Number of infirm detainees	987	1,052	1,172	1,394	1,647	1,672
Number of days' maintenance	1,505,393	1,619,176	1,685,076	1,714,064	1,825,798	1,801,170
Cost of maintenance	1,253,029 fr.	1,367,005 fr.	1,427,771 fr.	1,508,178 fr.	1,669,169 fr.	1,689,778 fr.
Average per head per day	83 c.	84 c.	85 c.	88 c.	91 c.	94 c.

Grouping the infirm with the able-bodied, therefore, the cost ranged from 8d. to 9d. per day during these years.

The cost of all inmates together, in 1905, worked out to £14 13s. 11d. per head, but the value of work done was equal to £5 7s. 5d., reducing the cost of the 3,500 able-bodied to £9 6s. 6d., or about 6d. per day. Of this, £3 7s. or 2½d. per day was paid in wages. By way of comparison it may be stated that, according to the Prison Commissioners, the cost of maintenance in English local prisons, after deducting the value of work done, is £22 11s., and that in convict prisons £28, but in these amounts no charge for buildings is included.

Perhaps the most remarkable feature of Merxplas is the facility of escape offered to the inmates and the frequency with which this facility is used. The escapes during the ten years 1898 to 1907 were as follows:—

1898   592

1899   565

1900   517

1901   769

1902   879

1903   1,004

1904   1,066

1905   1,243

1906   1,031

1907   919

As the figures already quoted show, a considerable proportion of the men who abscond are captured and sent back—though the number of escapes exceeded the recaptures by 112 in 1901, by 108 in 1902, by 120 in 1903, by 133 in 1904, by 146 in 1905, and by 107 in 1906—but those just given suggest plainly that a definite theory lies at the basis of the Director's usage in this matter. Escape is, in fact, judged very indulgently, and provided the man who gets away is found to have settled down to regular work no attempt is made to recapture him. In such a case it is the practice of the police to report to the Director, and if, during a period of six months, there is no fault to find with the absconder's conduct, he is pardoned; if otherwise, he is sent back to complete his sentence. This apparent laxity of administration is, after all, strictly in keeping with the object of the Colony, which is less to punish than to restrain under discipline, until that discipline has achieved its purpose, and the man is fit to regain his liberty—in the Director's favourite term, to be "reclassed" in society. If such reinstatement is expedited by act of the inmate's will, the aim of the establishment is no less served. I cannot do better than quote from an interesting letter upon this subject which Monsieur Stroobant has been kind enough to send me.

> "The inconveniences caused by the escape of prisoners," writes Monsieur Stroobant, "are in reality less than they might appear to be. Escapes take place in periods, and at certain epochs—for example, at the beginning of a new year, at carnival, at the return of the busy season, at the beginning of the month when wages have been paid. The gang which intends to escape exchanges paper money for coin which circulates clandestinely in the court yard; thus 1.50 franc paper money is only worth 1 franc outside. The exchange is higher according as the searches ordered by the administration are more frequent.

> "Most escapes take place amongst the agricultural labourers. About twenty-three gangs, each composed of from 60 to 100 men, work daily in the fields and the fir woods, everywhere a league away from the establishment. Each gang is accompanied by one warder and a sentinel only, hence these agricultural labourers have the greatest possible facility for escaping. Mainly, however, to the signals which are immediately given to the gendarmes, and to the special watch organised by the brigade of gendarmerie in the vicinity of the Colony, a large number of fugitives, recognised by clothing belonging to the establishment which they wear, are quickly recaptured. One may say, in general, that the fugitives of Merxplas are, as a rule, recaptured within fifteen hours of their escape. The men thus recaptured are punished with a fortnight's interment in cell, and are afterwards kept in closed quarters, from which it is impossible to escape again, for a number of months proportionate to their attempts to abscond. Persons guilty

of repeated attempts, who are confined in these closed quarters, receive reduced wages.

"The virtual certainty that they will be recaptured after a brief interval, the salutary fear of the punishment which awaits them, and the lack of proper clothing are reasons why the number of escapes is not far greater than is the case.

"Those who escape are the energetic men who, influenced by some ruling idea—it may be of a family in distress or other motives less laudable—seek to reclass themselves. They are not always, by any means, the most corrupt, and often when I learn, from a police report, that a fugitive is following regular work, I ask the Minister (of Justice) to suspend the order for his recapture.

"From the standpoint of the general security of the establishment, the facility of escape constitutes a valuable safety valve, which it is expedient to recognise. In truth, the latent energies which impel a man, at all costs, to seek emancipation from the bondage which he has to endure in the Beggars' Depot are exhausted by flight. If that alternative did not exist, the elements of frequent revolts would exist, and these would compel the administration to increase greatly the existing number of warders."

Probably owing to the fact that the yoke of bondage sits lightly on the inmates, serious insubordination is said to be exceptional. The following scale of punishments applies according to the gravity of the offence: (1) three to sixty days' simple cell detention with ordinary diet; (2) three days' detention in punishment cells with ordinary diet; (3) three days' ordinary cell detention with bread and water diet; (4) three days' detention in punishment cells with bread and water diet; (5) confinement in the punishment quarters for serious insubordination. Offenders may also be transferred to inferior classes of work. The punishments awarded in 1907 related to the following offences: Escapes and attempts to escape, 919; refusal to work or idleness at work, 250; malingering, 9; brawling, 60; rebellion against warders, 72; theft and complicity, 57; misconduct, 407; and drunkenness, 18. The small military guard is always at hand to quell disturbance, should it occur, but its services are never needed for this purpose.

The fact that between 80 and 90 per cent. of the inmates are habitual offenders proves that Merxplas does not repress vagrancy and mendicity, though that was the purpose in the mind of the authors of the law of 1891;

it does, however, relieve the country, at all times, of the fairly constant number of 4,000 loafers, and while public order and morality benefit, the cost to the community is very small. For the discipline of Merxplas proves that the loafer can work, and work well, if he chooses. Some words, on this subject, written by the Lindsey Committee deserve to be quoted:—

> "The men at Merxplas have retained a large proportion of whatever manual and technical skill they possessed when they first began to slip out of employment in the outside world. They have entered the colony before the rapid deterioration, which is the inevitable result of the tramp life, has had time to take effect, and the opportunity afforded them to practice their trades has, in most cases, prevented their ever sinking to the level of the average English tramp. In every shop the keen interest the men take in their work is most noticeable; only one foreman and one warder are employed in each shop, and without coercion the men seemed all working with remarkable energy and real interest. This is, in our opinion, perhaps the most striking feature of the whole establishment....
>
> "Inside, away from temptation, they work well, and as long as the sentence does not exceed two or three years, seem content to remain.... Even if permanent re-establishment in society is not frequently secured, this large class of the inefficients, which would otherwise form the great recruiting ground for the criminal classes, is prevented from sinking any lower. Its members are also prevented from propagating their kind, to prey upon the next generation. They have a decent and fairly comfortable life, which is largely self-supporting, and the cost is certainly far less than that of keeping them outside by the agency of charitable doles, interspersed with costly periods of residence in workhouse or gaol.
>
> "The workman slipping out of employment is there treated as a patient requiring care, not as a criminal requiring punishment, and his downward career is arrested before his technical skill is lost. The large amount of highly-skilled labour found there, compared to the utter incapacity of the average English prisoner committed for vagrancy, indicates the measure of the difference between the tramp at the commencement of his career and the same man after any lengthy period of life on the road. This skill may not indeed be sufficient to maintain the man outside, especially in face

of the drink difficulty, but it is undoubtedly sufficient, inside and in the aggregate, to make him nearly self-supporting and to give a real interest to his life. In addition to thus preserving a national asset of no inconsiderable value, the technical skill of the partly-efficient, the colony system subjects the whole vagrant class to the steadying influence of regular life and regular work for long periods of time. Even where this is insufficient to re-establish the man in independent life, the evidence of the Belgian colonies is emphatic that it is sufficient to make his life both profitable to the community and not unpleasant to himself. It also effectually safeguards his class both from drink and from the attractions of the criminal class, and it certainly largely checks its reproduction."

WORTEL HOUSE OF REFUGE.

The House of Refuge at Wortel may be regarded as a Detention Colony for the less obnoxious offenders of the vagrant and mendicant class, but it also receives persons who voluntarily enter owing to inability to find employment or homes. The House of Refuge thus performs the functions of the labour yard attached to many English workhouses, an institution useful, and even essential, in any well-organised system of poor relief so long as it is reserved for the proper people, and is used in order to meet purely temporary needs, instead of being converted into a device, as it often is, for evading the duty of seeking regular employment and for living permanently upon the rates.

The Colony is worked in two sections, Hoogstraeten and Wortel proper; at the former the helpless and sick are received, at the latter the able-bodied and those who, though infirm, are yet able to do light work. The maximum duration of detention, as has been explained, is one year, but any colonist may take his discharge directly he has saved 12s. from his earnings, or can show that he has work to go to. The average stay of able-bodied inmates is two or three months, but a certain number are allowed to remain beyond the year.

The following table shows the numbers who entered and left the Wortel House of Refuge in the years 1902 to 1908:—

	1902.	1903.	1904.	1905.	1906.	1907.	1908.
Admitted	4,389	3,428	3,546	3,057	2,505	2,402	2,798
Discharged	4,034	3,372	3,413	3,116	2,318	2,105	2,215
Discharged	177	138	142	135	125	152	142

Transferred	177	138	142	135	125	152	142
Absconded	85	72	40	58	59	91	118
Died	87	99	99	74	82	92	83
Total	4,383	3,681	3,694	3,383	2,584	2,440	2,558
Detained on December 31	2,003	1,750	1,602	1,276	1,197	1,159	1,399

The frequency of commitment during the same years was as follows:—

Number of Times Committed.	1901.	1902.	1903.	1904.	1905.	1906.	1907.	1908.
For the first time	1,523	1,483	1,281	1,296	1,070	903	856	1,222
For the second time	709	772	555	596	524	402	375	435
For the third time	413	478	380	389	320	232	234	261
For the fourth time	291	329	257	249	249	174	176	163
For the fifth time, or oftener	1,238	1,327	955	1,016	894	794	761	717
Total number of admissions	4,174	4,389	3,428	3,546	3,057	2,505	2,402	2,798

Both at Hoogstraeten and Wortel agriculture and industry are carried on; the trades at the former place include brewing, soap making, smithery, joinery, painting, stove making, cart building, and corn milling, and at the latter hand-loom weaving (cotton and woollen), tailoring, shoemaking, saddling, joinery and cabinet making, painting, smithery, and stove making. As far as possible, every man is put to the trade he knows best. The main aim is to produce articles which are needed for use or consumption in the Colony, and the surplus production is sold to other Government institutions. There are two farms, and besides the ordinary work provided by them, a certain amount of reclamation is done. Most of the building needed is the work of the colonists, and nearly all the domestic work is done by them.

The actual hours of labour, exclusive of intervals, are ten and a half daily in the summer months (April 1 to September 30), eight and a half in March and October, and eight in the winter months (November 1 to February 28). The daily routine is as follows (Sunday excepted):—

	March.	April 1 to September 30.	October.	November 1 to February 28.
Hour of Rising	5.30 a.m.	5.0 a.m.	5.30 a.m.	6.0 a.m.
Distribution of bread	6.0 "	5.30 "	6.0 "	6.30 "
Work	6.30 "	6.0 "	6.30 "	7.0 "
Visit of doctor	8.0 "	7.0 "	8.0 "	8.0 "
Distribution of coffee, and rest	9.0 "	8.0 "	9.0 "	[57] "
Work	9.15 "	8.30 "	9.15 "	—
Dinner, and rest	12.0 "	12.0 "	12.0 "	12.0 "
Work	1.30 p.m.	1.30 p.m.	1.30 p.m.	1.30 p.m.
Rest	3.0 "	4.0 "	3.0 p.m.	—
Work	3.15 "	4.30 "	3.15 p.m.	—
Cessation of work[58]	5.0 "	7.0 "	5.0 "	4.30 "
Supper	5.0 "	7.0 "	5.0 "	5.0 "
Bedtime	6.0 "	7.30 "	6.0 "	6.0 "

There is a regular scale of money payments, ranging from 9 centimes to 71 centimes per day, according to the class of work and of worker. The following are the daily rates now in force (100 centimes = 9½d.):—

	Class A. Centimes.	Class B. Centimes.	Class C. Centimes.
Workshops, etc.	47-71	24-47	24
Cultivation, plantation, and navvies' work	42-60	21-42	21
Domestic and agricultural	18-27	9-18	9

Of their earnings one-third is paid to the inmates at once and the balance is given to them on discharge.

The costs of maintenance payable by the public authorities which send colonists to Wortel are: For able-bodied persons 7½d. per day, for those not able-bodied 7½d. if they do not require special attention, and 1s. 2½d. if they do.

By the admission of the officials of the Wortel Colony the permanent effect of detention upon the character and life of the persons interned is small. This would appear to be proved, indeed, by the return of recommitments, which shows that of the inmates received in 1907 and 1908 over 64 and 56 per cent. respectively were recidivists. It is held that the weak points about the method of treatment are the lightness of the discipline and the shortness of the term of detention. While the maximum term of detention is twelve months, the conditions of discharge are so easy that the average stay is only two or three months, a period far too short to influence permanently the idle and dissolute who form the larger proportion of the inmates. Moreover, many of the latter are confirmed inebriates, needing a special treatment, which is impossible in an institution of this kind.

A few words may be added here relative to the Forced Labour Colonies of Holland. These Colonies are of the type found in Belgium, and their mode of working is in general the same. As in Belgium, too, they were originally administered by a Benevolent Society, which was formed about the year 1818 for the establishment of Beggars' Colonies, Voluntary Colonies for free farmers and labourers, and Colonies for old and infirm people and for orphans. To this end an estate of moorland, about 1,200 acres in extent, was acquired, but further purchases increased the area to 13,430 acres, of which 2,900 acres were allotted to the Free Colonies, 1,250 acres to the Veterans' Colonies, and 4,280 acres to the Beggars' Colonies, the remaining 5,000 acres being moorland. The Beggars' Colonies were handed over to the State in 1859, but two Free Colonies are still continued by the same society at Frederiksoord and Willemsoord, and to them two classes of people are admitted: (1) free farmers, who are encouraged to remain permanently on small holdings provided for them on easy terms; and (2) free labourers, who work on the home farms of the Colony, and who, if married, live in separate cottages, and, with such members of their families as can work, are paid wages at a rate lower than that for outside labour.

At the present time there are three Penal Colonies under State administration—at Veenhuizen and Hoorn for men, and at Leyden for women; all of them are intended for the reception of vagrants and mendicants, and the men's Colonies also receive habitual drunkards.

In addition to agriculture, gardening, and forestry, various trades, such as weaving, carpentering, masonry, smithery, cabinet making, shoe making, and tailoring, are carried on. The buildings have been modernised, and the cubicle system of dormitory is almost universally adopted. Wages are paid to the men as at Merxplas, and the unexpended balance is handed to them on discharge.

CHAPTER V.

THE GERMAN LABOUR HOUSES.

The early legislation of Germany relative to begging and vagrancy was not greatly dissimilar in spirit from our own. Down to the sixteenth century Germany was satisfied with the mere prohibition of these practices. A Resolution of the Diet at Lindau in 1497 simply forbade vagabondage, and ordered the authorities to exercise supervision over beggars of all kinds. In 1532 Emperor Charles V., in Article 30 of his Penal Court Ordinance, similarly enjoined the authorities to "exercise vigilant oversight over beggars and vagrants," and in 1557 the Imperial Police Ordinance sanctioned the issue of begging letters to poor people for whose support local funds did not exist.

During the eighteenth century a series of decrees and regulations were issued against begging in various German States, but without suppressing it, and towards the end of the century the evil in many parts of the country had reached proportions which threatened public security.

> "As late as the third quarter of the eighteenth century, and in some parts of the country until its close, the most shameless and wide-spread mendicity defied at once the severest official prohibitions and the best meant endeavour of the communes and private individuals."[59]

Then it was that the idea of the disciplinary treatment of vagrants and loafers in general took root, leading in time to the institution all over the country of special houses of detention, not inaptly called Labour Houses, for the reception of these offenders, of the work-shy of every description, and of certain other classes of people who followed a disorderly mode of life. When the Empire was established, the practice of the various States was embodied in the Imperial Penal Code, and Labour House treatment is now the recognised mode of correcting sloth, loafing, and habitual intemperance and immorality throughout Germany.

Sections 361 and 362 of the Penal Code define as follows the offences which may entail detention in a Labour House:—

> "(1) Whoever wanders about as a vagabond.
>
> "(2) Whoever begs or causes children to beg or neglects to restrain from begging such persons as are under his control and oversight and belong to his household.
>
> "(3) Whoever is so addicted to gambling, drunkenness, or idleness that he falls into such a condition as to be

compelled to seek public help himself, or for those for whose maintenance he is responsible.

"(4) Any female who is placed under police control owing to professional immorality when she acts contrary to the police regulations issued in the interest of health, public order, and public decency, or who, without being under such control, is guilty of professional immorality.

"(5) Any person who, while in receipt of public relief, refuses out of sloth to do such work suited to his strength as the authorities may offer him.

"(6) Any person who, after losing his past lodging, fails to procure another within the time allotted to him by the competent authority and who cannot prove that in spite of his best endeavours he has been unable to do so."

An Amendment of the Penal Code dated June 25, 1900, added to this list of offenders procurers and *souteneurs*. The law enjoins that persons convicted of misdemeanours as above may be handed over to the State police authorities after undergoing the allotted imprisonment, with a view to their further detention in Labour Houses, there to be usefully employed under strict control. Some of the Prussian Labour Houses are used, to a small extent, for the reception of youths who are taken from parental control owing to bad behaviour.

The mode of procedure under this law is very summary, but very effectual. A vagrant, a loafer, or a work-shirker falls into the hands of the policeman, who in Germany is taught to protect both the highway and the street against uses for which they were never intended. By this official he is haled before the *Amtsgericht*, which is a local Court of First Instance for the adjudication of petty cases. As a rule, he is sentenced to a few weeks' imprisonment, and to be afterwards handed over to the *Landespolizei* or State Police Authority. In effect, he is despatched to the district in which the original offence was committed. The whole of the documents in the case are passed on to the President or Prefect of this district, and it is this official who fixes the term of detention in the provincial Labour House. The maximum period is two years, but whether the man obtains discharge at the end of a shorter sentence depends entirely upon himself. If he shows distinct signs of improvement as the result of his discipline, he may be released. If not the sentence is probably prolonged for six months, or in bad cases to the maximum term, at the end of which the prisoner must unconditionally be discharged, whether reformed or not. In practice it rests entirely with the Director of the Labour House to determine whether a sentence should be prolonged or not, for though the District President nominally decides, it is on the direct representation of the Director, whose recommendation is seldom or never ignored.

Thus, the Labour House is not punitive in the technical sense; it exists for the one purpose of training the lazy and the vicious to a life of labour and industry. Labour Houses of this kind are found in almost all the States, in numbers proportionate to the population. Some of them, however, serve for large towns, as in the case of Berlin, Hamburg, and Dresden. Prussia has twenty-five Labour Houses, of which seven are for men only, two for women only, and sixteen for both sexes. The following is a list of these institutions, with the accommodation they afforded in the year 1908:—

GERMAN LABOUR HOUSES.

Labour House. (Locality)	Province	Accommodation for Detainees.		Wards.		Number of			Cells and Cabins.
		Males.	Females.	Males.	Females.	Dormitories.	Workrooms.	Sickrooms.	
Tapiau	East Prussia	392	80	—	—	11	9	6	23
Konitz	West Prussia	350	100	170	100	16	8	13	13
Rummelsburg	Brandenburg	400	300	225	75	20	30	20	—
Strausberg	"	380	—	90	—	10	41	9	—
Prenzlau	"	400	—	80	26	9	23	12	12
Landsberg a. W.	"	190	40	50	30	7	37	15	3
Neustettin	Pomerania	150	10	40	20	9	11	13	—
Ückermünde	"	340				14	7	7	2
Stralsund	"	120	25	—	—	5	4	4	—
Greifswald	"	110	—	—	—	3	4	—	—
Bojanowo	Posen	450	—	—	—	2	26	8	—
Fraustadt	"	—	130	—	—	4	5	3	—

Schweidnitz	Silesia	1,200	150	130	50	46	64	16	13
Breslau	"	600	300	—	—	22	17	8	2
Gross Salze	Saxony	358	57	90	30	18	39	16	21
Moritzburg	"	505	55	8	2	14	35	10	19
Glückstadt	Schleswig	700	50	—	—	15	27	5	19
Bockelholm	"	300	—	—	—	2	6	3	—
Benninghausen	Westphalia	350	60	—	—	21	23	6	3
Breitenau	Hesse-Nassau	300	35	30	5	5	14	4	—
Hadamar	"	236	80	10	6	9	12	5	—
Brauweiler	Rhine Province	1,090	195	50	105	47	56	16	281
Moringen	Hanover	800	—	—	—	21	27	14	16
Wunstorf	"	300	—	550	—	22	26	37	103
Himmelsthür	"	—	125	—	190	10	7	11	29

The numbers of persons, detained for correction, dealt with by the whole of the Prussian Labour Houses in the course of the administrative year 1907-8 were as follows:—

	Males	Females	Total
Number at the beginning of the year	7.200	848	8,048
Admitted during the year	6,716	731	7,447
Discharged during the year	6,839	892	7,731

	Males	Females	Total
Number at the end of the year	7,077	687	7,764
Total number detained	13,916	1,579	15,495
Average number detained daily	6,779	749	7,528

The persons detained were classified in the following groups of occupations:—

	Males	Females	Total
Agriculture, forestry, gardening, fishing, etc.	923	30	953
Industry, mining, and building trades	3,057	42	3,099
Trade and commerce	717	17	734
Domestic service and casual labour	1,488	296	1,784
Public service and professions	114	5	119
No occupation, or none declared	8	302	310
Totals	6,307	629	6,999

Of 6,990 persons classified by age, 174 were under twenty-one years of age, 262 were from twenty-one to twenty-five years of age, 529 from twenty-five to thirty, 1,664 from thirty to forty, 2,231 from forty to fifty, 1,532 from fifty to sixty, 548 from sixty to seventy, and 50 were seventy years of age and upwards.

The offences for which 6,299 male and 692 female inmates were committed to the Labour Houses in that year were as follows:—

	Males	Females	Total
Vagabondage	328	47	375
Begging	4,166	69	4235
Begging and vagrancy together	702	31	733
Laziness	97	6	103
Professional immorality	188	481	669
Work-shyness	8	3	11
Homelessness	810	55	865
Totals	5,299	692	6,991

The periods of commitment by the judicial authorities were as under:—

	Males	Females	Total
Three months or less	20	5	25
From three to six months	1,443	242	1,685
Over six months and under two years	3,535	359	3,594
Two years	1,599	85	1,684
Total	6,297	691	6,988

Of the offenders enumerated above, 4,445 or 64 per cent. had been detained in a Labour House before, and 2,293 or 33 per cent. had been so detained more than three times, while 5,865 or 84 per cent. had been in prison. Further, 1,253 or 18 per cent. had been recommitted to a Labour House within twelve months of their last discharge from the same.

Most of these Labour Houses are situated in the open country, and follow a mixed economy of agriculture and industry, though the number of men who can be employed usefully in farm work would appear to be small. The following statement of the different modes of employment in force in 1908 comprises young people detained for reformation, in addition to the adults committed by judicial process for disciplinary reasons:—

EMPLOYMENT OF DETAINEES.

	Males	Females	Total
Average daily number of detainees	8,775	1,275	10,050
Average daily number employed	7,290	904	8,194
Character of employment—			
1. For the Labour Houses—			
(a) Domestic work	1,524	372	1,896
(b) Agriculture	551	32	583
(c) Other work	642	85	727
Total (a), (b), (c)	2,717	489	3,206
2 For the Provincial Authorities	1,903	88	1,991
3. For the Public Authorities	105	—	105

4. For officers of the establishments	124	23	147
5. For outside persons—			
(*a*) Agricultural	704	21	725
(*b*) Industrial work	1,737	283	2,020
Total (*a*), (*b*)	2,441	304	2,745

In considering the industrial methods on which the Labour Houses are administered, it may be well to bear in mind the principles which are applied to Prussian penal establishments in general, for they apply to these institutions. A recent official statement upon the subject runs as follows[60]:—

> "(1) The requirements of the individual establishments, and of the prison administration in general, are as far as possible to be supplied by the prisoners. All domestic work is to be done by the prisoners; clothing and articles needed for bedding, etc., are also to be done by them, and to this end weaving shops are provided in some prisons. Repairs to buildings, works of rebuilding, extensions, and new buildings are to be carried out by prisoners, who are specially to be used in the construction of dwelling-houses for the officers.
>
> "(2) The production of useful articles needed by the Imperial and State authorities is to be encouraged as far as possible, and this branch of work increases every year. Tailoring and other equipment work for barracks and hospitals are largely done to the order of the War Office, also furniture for official rooms for the State Railway Administrations.
>
> "(3) Criminal prisoners may be used for agricultural improvement works on behalf of State and communal authorities, and also of private persons, provided at least a year of their sentence has expired, their conduct has been good, and the remainder of their sentence does not exceed a year, or in exceptional cases two years. With their consent correctional prisoners who have served six months (and in

exceptional cases three months), have been of good behaviour, and have not longer than two years to serve, may be similarly employed. Criminal and correctional prisoners may not be employed together; and they must be kept apart from free workmen. In order to prevent injury to free labour prisoners may only be employed in the manner stated if the works in question would not otherwise be executed for lack of free labourers, or because the high wages of the latter would make the works unprofitable. Under the same conditions, prisoners may be put to agricultural work. These works are done in all the provinces of the Kingdom, and the following works are executed in particular:—

> "(a) Moor land is cultivated in order to the settlement of farmers. Thus the reclamation of the Augstumal Moor, in East Prussia, 3,000 hectares (7,410 acres) in extent, is in an advanced state, and seventeen settlers have already been established there and provided with houses. The Kehding Moor, in the Stade district, has now been prepared for settlement, and five colonists are established. The Bargstedt Moor is so far reclaimed that settlers may now be taken; fifteen holdings of 12 hectares (30 acres) each are contemplated. In the Eifel district 75 hectares (185 acres) of the High Venn plateau, over 2,200 feet high, have been cultivated, and the first settlers established.

> "(b) Shifting sand dunes are made permanent.

> "(c) Marshy ground is drained, damage done by inundations is made good, water courses are diverted, and channels dug.

> "(d) Fiscal domains are put into an efficient condition.

> "(e) Vineyards are planted for the State on the Moselle.

"Experience has proved that prisoners can best be employed on such works in gangs of from forty to sixty, under a chief overseer, assisted by a sufficient number of warders." "The prisoners," says the official document, show themselves to be willing, diligent, and apt in their work; their productivity is inferior to that of free labourers only at the beginning of their employment, and later it is equal. There is no difficulty in maintaining discipline, and attempts at escape occur very seldom. On the other hand the employment of small bodies of men under the superintendence of one or two petty officers, especially if it be in agricultural work, in which it is almost impossible to prevent contact with free labourers, leads to serious abuses:—bribery, insubordination, rebellion against the officers and even gross acts of violence have occurred. Such small bodies of men, therefore, can only be employed in exceptional cases where the conditions for the maintenance of discipline are specially favourable.

"(4) The other prisoners are to be farmed to *entrepreneurs* by public contract for the carrying on of industrial work. Care must be taken, however, that too many prisoners are not allotted to a single employer, and that the number employed in a single industry is not disproportionate to the number of free labourers engaged in the same industry. Since 1869, the number of prisoners employed by industrial *entrepreneurs* fell from 73 to 27·2 per cent. in 1903,[61] and a further decrease is probable owing to the extension of the work done for the State authorities. Several establishments have entirely discontinued the employment of prisoners in that way. By the restriction of factory work, the individuality of the prisoner can be better studied in the choice of employment for them, and the justification is taken away from the complaints made by free workpeople about the illegitimate competition of cheap prison labour, used by capitalist employers. At the same time, the prison budgets are less satisfactory than formerly as a consequence."

In the prison accounts no allowance is made for the domestic and farm work done by the prisoners. In calculating the value of all work done for the Imperial and State authorities and for the general Prison Administration wages are reckoned at 40 pfennige (5d.) per head per day.

"This rate of wages, which is far less than that paid by employers, is taken arbitrarily, but in order to simplify the trade accounts and particularly accounts with the various State authorities, a uniform rate was necessary. If the rate is low, the Prison Administration must console itself with the reflection that its losses imply saving to other branches of the State service; the State, as a whole, does not suffer injury. Moreover, the full value of the prisoners' work now goes to the State, and not as formerly to private employers, and free labour no longer suffers from the competition of prison work."[62]

Wages ranging, according to capacity and diligence, from 1 to 20 pfennige (100 pfennige =1s.) per day in the case of criminal prisoners, and from 1 to 30 pfennige per day in the case of correctional prisoners, are credited to the men, with the object of giving them a favourable restart in life on their discharge. No part of the accumulated bonuses is paid over during imprisonment until 30s. has been earned by criminal prisoners, and 20s. by others, except that payments may be made to a man's family out of his account; but one half of all earnings beyond the minimum stated may be used in the purchase of extra food, books, clothing, etc., though not of tobacco, the smoking of which is not allowed.

The following statement gives the yearly cost per head in the financial year April 1, 1907, to March 31, 1908, of the whole of the inmates of the Prussian Labour Houses, with the value per head of the produce and work done and the amount per head which fell upon the public funds:—

Labour House. (Locality)	Yearly Cost per Head of Average Number of Detainees.		How the Cost was Covered.			
			(a) By Produce of the Labour House.		(b) Public Contributions.	
	Mark.	Pfennige.	Mark.	Pfennige.	Mark.	Pfennige.
Tapiau	642	51	302	64	339	87
Konitz	383	27	204	46	178	81
Rummelsburg	507	21	124	21	383	0
Strausberg	434	0	215	0	219	0
Prenzlau	547	15	280	46	266	69

Landsberg a. W.	401	41	234	83	166	58
Neustettin	442	68	268	24	174	44
Uckermüode	406	31	221	54	184	77
Stralsund	480	77	361	05	119	72
Greifswald	340	0	220	29	119	71
Bojanowo	355	45	172	14	183	31
Fraustadt	694	49	145	23	549	26
Schweidnitz	313	40	255	17	58	23
Breslau	674	32	625	17	49	15
Gross Salze	339	29	271	54	67	75
Moritzburg	344	76	271	01	73	75
Glückstadt	425	26	410	42	14	84
Bockelholm	355	30	222	02	133	28
Benninghausen	498	76	153	85	344	91
Breitenau	453	84	397	70	56	14
Hadamar	278	80	140	99	137	81
Brauweiler	396	68	271	97	124	71
Moringen	791	09	142	0	649	09
Wunstorf	377	61	131	64	245	97
Himmelsthür	363	42	159	13	204	29

It appears from this statement that the gross annual cost per head ranged from £13 18s 10d. in the case of the Labour House at Hadamar (a small institution) to £39 11s. at the Labour House at Moringen, and that the net cost to the State ranged from 14s. 10d. per head in the case of the Labour House at Glückstadt to £32 9s. at Moringen.

CHAPTER VI.

A GERMAN TRAMP PRISON.[63]

The German method of dealing with vagrants and loafers may be studied in its practical details with great advantage by visiting the Labour House of Benninghausen, in the Prussian Province of Westphalia. The establishment is situated in the open country, ten or twelve miles distant from the old town of Soest, and its high boundary walls and spiked fences enclose an area of about twelve English acres. The nearest railway station is four or five miles away, and the visitor's first impression is that of a sparsely populated country, in which the prisoners who from time to time manage to elude the eye of their warders can have but little chance of successful flight. The Labour House was built in 1821 to accommodate 410 persons, and it is administered by the Government of the Province. The books of the establishment value the land at £1,022, while the buildings are insured for £19,950, and the furniture, equipment, and material for £5,329.

Benninghausen is an admirable example of the application of the allopathic principle to penology. As sloth is the vice which brings the majority of prisoners within its walls, so rigorous exertion is the method of cure that is followed. The House is the veriest hive of industry. The idea would never occur to you that these groups of diligent workers, engaged in all sorts of useful crafts and employments, were not long ago wandering aimlessly about the country cherishing the delusive idea that work was beneath contempt, and that the dignity of man consists in requiring someone else to tie your bootlaces. Yet one important principle is strictly followed—whatever the work done, it is not allowed to compete with the free labour market. Hence, efforts are first directed to the provision of every possible need of the Labour House itself and of its inhabitants. This applies not only to the provision of food, but also to the weaving of materials, the making of iron and woodwork, the carrying out of repairs, and other matters of domestic economy. Beyond that the similar needs of other provincial institutions—like the Asylums for the Sick, for the Imbeciles, for the Blind, and for the Deaf and Dumb—are supplied as the convenience of the Labour House allows. This is all done, of course, on a business footing. An accurate account is taken of the labour employed, and the wages of this labour, reckoned on a moderate scale, plus the cost of material and a slight profit to cover contingencies, constitute the price charged by the Director for the goods he sells.

The Province of Westphalia is overwhelmingly Roman Catholic, but as the Benninghausen Labour House is the only one in the province it has to be conducted on what is known as the "paritative" basis; it serves for both confessions, though each has its special chaplain. At the time of my visit the institution was housing temporarily, in addition to the ordinary subjects of correction, a number of lads and girls, the children of abandoned parents, the charge of whom had been undertaken by the Poor Law Authority in virtue of the law of 1890, and for whom more suitable provision did not exist at the moment.

The numbers of detainees dealt with during the financial year 1907-8 were as follows:—

	Males	Females	Total
Number on April 1	307	27	334
Admitted during year	377	25	402
Discharged during year	329	30	359
Remained, March 31	355	22	377
Total number dealt with during year	684	52	736
Daily average number	367	23	330
Maximum number	355	27	—
Minimum number	280	20	—

Those committed in 1907-8 had committed the following offences:—

	Males	Females	Total
Vagabondage	25	—	25

Begging	29	1	277
Begging and vagabondage together	29	—	29
Idleness	16	—	16
Work-shyness	2	—	2
Homelessness	16	—	16
Professional immorality	9	27	36

Of the men newly admitted, 177 had been detained in a Labour House before, 64 of them more than three times, and the great majority had been imprisoned.

Structurally, the Labour House is not, perhaps, a model of what such an institution might and should be in these days, nor is this surprising when it is remembered that it has stood now for three generations, yet its arrangements are, within the limits determined by space and the architectural ideas of ninety years ago, excellent, and they are certainly excellently supervised. There are three separate blocks of buildings. The principal one contains the administrative rooms, the day-rooms, the dormitories, baths, and kitchens. Separate departments, without contact of any kind, are provided for the sexes, the women being lodged on the ground floor and the men above. The second block contains the workrooms, of which there are five, besides the large bakery and washhouses, *viz.*, a workshop for joiners and carpenters, one for weaving, one for cigar making, one for shoe making and a smithy and machine shop. The third building is the hospital, and is sufficiently isolated. This is not intended, however, for the chronically sick, who, with the physically disabled, are transferred, on medical certificate, to the Provincial Poorhouse and Hospital. Cases of child-birth are removed betimes to the Maternity Hospital, and the mothers afterwards return to the Labour House to complete their terms of imprisonment.

The bedrooms are plain yet light and cheerful apartments, not over-large, but as fresh and airy as an abundance of open windows can make them. Each prisoner has his own little iron bedstead, with straw pallet and pillow, and a coloured counterpane, and his name is boldly written at the head. The utmost care is taken to lodge the prisoners according to age, character, and characteristics. "We have separate bedrooms for the old, the middle-aged, and the young, separate rooms also for the first offenders and for the recidivists," said the Labour Inspector who showed me round the institution, "for we study peculiarities as much as possible. We also study their comfort," he added, "for we put all the snorers together."

The day begins for the inmates at 4.30 during the summer months (April 1 to September 30), and at 5.30 during winter and on Sundays and festivals. The hours are divided as follows:—

> 4.30 a.m.—At the sound of the bell every prisoner has to rise, dress, and wash, and in a quarter of an hour must have arranged his bedclothes and be ready to leave the dormitory.
>
> 4.45 a.m.—Assembling in the corridors the prisoners are numbered, after which (so runs the "Order of the Day"), "they shall offer up at word of command (*auf Commando*) a silent prayer." Then the field labourers, the implement room workers, and the bakers go to the dining rooms, and the weavers, tailors, shoemakers, cigar makers, and the female inmates to the workrooms, there to begin at once their work.
>
> 4.50 a.m.—The bell sounds for the morning meal (soup and bread), the inmates going to the same in bands in charge of the overseers.
>
> 9.0 a.m.—Work is then continued without interruption until 9.0, when there is a pause for a quarter of an hour for bread and beer.
>
> 11.40 a.m.—A pause for dinner, which is partaken like breakfast in bands. (For the outside labourers a different order is followed.)
>
> 12.0 to 1.0 p.m.—A pause, during which the prisoners have at least half an hour in the open air.
>
> 4.0 p.m.—A pause of a quarter of an hour for bread and beer.
>
> 7.15 p.m. (in winter and on Sundays and festivals, 6.15).—The bell rings for supper, and work ends for the day.

> 7.50 p.m.—The prisoners are examined for the detection of forbidden articles, and at 7.55 they are marched off to bed.

The work-day is thus about twelve hours in summer. But while, as a rule, the hours are the same for all, work is not altogether measured by time, but according to the capacity of the individual inmate, and where the tasks imposed are unfulfilled at the close of the day, owing to evident sloth or insubordination, some sort of punishment follows.

The dietary on ordinary work-days is as follows:—

> Morning.—Coffee with milk and bread.
>
> Noon.—Peas, beans, or lentils with potatoes; vegetable soup with potatoes; cabbage or turnips, with potatoes (the portion of potatoes allowed is 750 grammes for men and 660 grammes for women); or fresh fish and potatoes.
>
> Evening.—Soup, made with rye or wheaten flour, bread, oats, buckwheat, rice or potatoes. (Of bread 550 grammes are allowed to each man and 400 grammes to each woman daily). At Easter, Whitsuntide, Christmas, and on the Emperor's birthday, beef or pork, with beer, is given. Twice a week 100 grammes of meat may be served to men, and 80 grammes to women, instead of the fat which enters into the noon meal. Once a week cheese (100 grammes) is served to men and women, and once also a salted herring.

The whole of the prisoners are kept to work of a kind suited to their strength, capacity and sex, their employment being determined by the Director and the resident doctor together. The principal methods of employment are the following:—

(1) Farm work on the provincial estate at Eichelborn, for which purpose men are farmed out as required.

(2) Building and earth works in connection with provincial institutions and undertakings.

(3) A series of industries carried on within the walls of the house.

(4) Works on the buildings, both within and without.

(5) Domestic and culinary work such as baking, washing, cleaning, sewing, etc.

The baking alone is a very serious task, for a thousand mouths have to be fed every day, since the two large ovens provide, not only for the Labour House itself, but for two other large public institutions situated not far away. In the weaving shop there are fourteen hand-looms for linen, the yarn for which is bought. The work done by the carpenters is various and thoroughly creditable. Furniture in request for provincial institutions is chiefly made, such as tables, benches, chests, chairs, toilette tables, and the like, and some of the work I saw would compare with the best products of free labour. "We have just sent out an account for £2,000 worth of goods," said the labour master with pride. The business of cigar making is not, like the other departments, carried on by the Labour House on its own account. The plan adopted is for labour to be farmed to tobacco manufacturers, who send the raw material with a skilled overseer to direct the various processes of preparation. The administration undertakes no responsibility for the quality of the work done, or for the material spoiled, though, on the other hand, the wages charged to the manufacturer are very low, *viz.*, 75 pfennige or 9d. per day. The various employments detailed in a recent official report included locksmithry, joinery and carpentry, basket and chair making, tinning, mason's work, roofing, painting and plastering, weaving and spooling, tailoring, boot and shoe making, saddlery, hair sorting, book-binding, cigar making, machine turning, repairs to tools and implements, copying, manifolding, baking, butchery, knitting, sewing, laundry work, farm and field work, and road making. The weaving department produced 45,547 metres of stuff, the tailoring department produced 158 complete suits and 2,890 single garments, the sewing department 5,099 bed coverlets, towels, shirts, aprons, handkerchiefs, neckerchiefs, etc.; the shoe making department 748 pairs of shoes, the carpentry department 1,319 articles of furniture, and so forth. The total value of the goods produced and of the labour farmed during the year was £6,164, which more than covered the cost of food and clothing.

Formerly the Labour House had its own farm, but this was separated some years ago, and it has since been conducted as an independent undertaking, though still by the aid of forced labour. Men are lent to the farm manager as required, at the rate of 60 pfennige or 7d. a day of ten or twelve hours, according to the season, and some forty or fifty are always employed in one way or other on the land. The Labour House buys its rye for bread, its milk, its butter, and its potatoes from the farm management at the full market prices, though, on the other hand, it sells to the farm all the implements of iron and wood which it is capable of supplying, and also makes its repairs.

In the year 1907-8 of an average *personnel* of 330, there were employed in domestic and other work for the institution 152 persons, while 142 were employed on work for the Provincial Administration, 50 were employed by outside persons in farm, industrial, and other work, and 10 worked for officers of the Labour House.

The entire cost in that financial year was £24 18s. 9d. per head, this sum including food, clothing, materials, and administration, and of the total expenditure the prisoners earned by their labour £7 13s. 10d. per head, leaving a deficit of £17 4s. 11d. per head, equal to 6s. 7½d. per week, to be made up by the Province. As compared with several years ago, there was an increase in both the gross and the net cost.

There is absolutely no contact between the workers of the several trade departments, for all save the bakers work behind locked doors, whose small windows only the officials may approach. The work, too, is strenuous in the full meaning of that hackneyed word. Every man literally works ever in his taskmasters eye; and not only so, but he must complete each day the task which is allotted to him. According to his capacity, and the character of his employment, a fixed *pensum* is required of him, and unless this is done there is a penalty to pay; while, on the other hand, to the industrious, who exceed the inevitable minimum of effort and output, a small reward is offered. The latter only ranges from a farthing to a penny a day, though by the accretions of a year it may grow into a sum which proves a welcome help to a man on his discharge. This accumulating bonus is, as a rule, kept intact until the time of discharge comes, when it is handed to the Police Authority of the place to which the man elects to go, to be paid to him in instalments or otherwise used advantageously on his behalf.

The women's department does not need particular description. It is conducted quite independently of the men's, though, of course, under the same higher officials, and its inmates are put to occupations suitable to their capacity and strength, not a small part of their time naturally being taken up by the domestic, culinary, and other indoor work inseparable from so large an establishment. In this department are found many members of a class which is one of the saddest excrescences of our modern urban life. These women of evil profession are, as a rule, detained in the Labour House for six months after the expiration of their gaol sentence. On discharge they are sent to their legal domicile if without fixed home or regular means of subsistence, but if they cannot establish a legal settlement they are handed over to the Poor Law Authority. It may be noted, however, that Germany does not as yet go as far as certain cantons of democratic Switzerland in the restraint of those single women of known moral weakness, so well known to English Poor Law workers, whose periodical visits to the workhouse imply an ever increasing burden on the public funds. Such persons the Berne Poor Law Authorities, for example, keep under duress indefinitely without the slightest misgiving that the sacred principle of individual liberty, in whose misused name so many wrongs to society and the commonwealth are committed, is being infringed. In Germany, as in England, these persons may, indeed, come under the restraining influence of the Poor Law when physically or intellectually defective, but for the rest the only power of detention resides in the penal provisions applicable, as above shown, to females found guilty of professional solicitation, a class to which most of the moral breakages which find their way into the women's wards of our own workhouses do not in the least belong.

Formal prison discipline is enforced in the Labour House at Benninghausen as in others. Possibly the purple patches of relaxation which variegate the lives of the inmates are too few and too far between. Here, however, the German authorities doubtless act according to the teaching of experience, and no one will doubt that a theory—whether satisfactory or not—lies at the basis of their practice. Sunday is, of course, a free day, and the high festivals of the Church are observed by the prisoners of both confessions and of none. Then a great quiet falls upon this house of toil. Black clothes become the order of the day, even to the soft round cap which covers the close-cropped head, and as often as the church-going bell sounds, the inmates are led to and from religious service. For the rest the time is divided between workshop, bed, and board—and unless the rules are scrupulously observed there is a good deal of board about the bed.

It goes without saying that the men are treated humanely and justly, but of indulgence there is no pretence, and I confess that as this aspect of Labour House discipline created upon my mind its own clear and vivid impression, I recalled that saying of Prince Bismarck, when he laid down the law of courtesy, "Politeness even to the murderer, but hang him all the same." I do not, however, presume to criticise the *régime* followed; may be it is the best for the people who pass beneath it. It is the serious side of life, rather than its levities and *insouciance*, which they need specially to know. Why should the tramp have all the ease and the honest worker all the hardships of life? It sounds like the refinement of cruelty, but in this land of Gargantuan smokers not only is the consoling companionship of tobacco forbidden to the mass of prisoners, but even the cigar makers themselves fall under the general ban, and may not test the result of their own deft handiwork.

Severe punishment is very seldom necessary, and Benninghausen does not possess the provision for treating acts of extreme misdemeanour which is to be found in some other German Labour Houses. "Arrest" in various grades is the worst penalty awarded. That means imprisonment in a dark cell, with bare boards for a bed and bread and water for diet. Even here, however, every fourth day brings respite and is, for that reason, known as a "good day" (*guter Tag*), for on it the prisoner may again, for one brief space, taste the joy of his accustomed straw pallet, while, to comfort or to tantalise him, he is also given warm food. But it is a fugitive bliss, for next day the pallet goes and warm food with it, and the erring one sleeps again on the floor and quenches his thirst at the water tap. A short time before my visit eight or ten of the incorrigible young "foster-children" of whom I have spoken had escaped from the Labour House while returning from church. A hue and cry was promptly raised, and in a couple of hours they were recaptured. They were birched for their escapade, for under the law referred to above the parental authority is transferred to the public foster parents, even to the extent of the right to inflict due bodily chastisement. With such exceptions, corporal punishment is unknown in the Labour House. The punishment for the loafer, the idler, and the tramp is hard work, and about its genuineness there can be no doubt whatever. But what would you otherwise? It is work which these men need, and want of it which has been their undoing. Look at it in that way. The Labour House is in effect a Continuation School. In it the hapless sons of the commonwealth who have failed to learn the lesson of industry in their early years are enabled to make good this important deficiency in their education. It is also coercive. Just as Germany applies compulsion in the instruction of adults who have failed to master their R's betimes, so it applies compulsion in imparting to the thriftless and shiftless members of society the spirit and habit of orderliness, industry, and self-control.

No one who has been inside a Tramp Prison can fail to detect the beneficial influence of rigid discipline upon the physique and bearing of these tramps and loafers of yesterday and the day before. It was hard to believe that the gangs of smart-looking men, who briskly deployed in the quadrangle in their clattering wooden shoes, were members of the same slouching brotherhood whose favourite haunt is the King's highway. One little scene, enacted all in a moment before my eyes, would have done credit to a drill-ground. A band of prisoners were returning along the quadrangle from exercise to their work, a warder behind them. Arrived at the doorway of the workshop, they halted dead at signal, fell into two lines, and stood motionless at attention with the rigidity and solemnity of a military watch, while the warder ponderously passed between them and led the way into the building. For they can, after all, be galvanised into life and vigour, into agility and alertness, these licensed drones of the commonwealth, these worthless hangers-on of the street corner and the highway, whom we are accustomed to regard as "finished and finite clods" whose betterment only a miracle could compass; all that is needed is the will to override their weakness and make them men in spite of themselves.

It may be asked, however, what is the practical effect of Labour House discipline on the after life of those who have experienced it? That a large proportion are won to a regular life of industry cannot, unfortunately, be said, nor would it be expected. In proof of this self-evident admission stands the patent fact that many of the inmates are recidivists who have been in and out of the Labour House time after time. Questioned on the point the Director placed the percentage of genuine reformations at 25, and the proportion of those who are directly benefited, without being actually reclaimed, at from a third to a half of the whole. "One half at the outside," was his most sanguine estimate, volunteered, I must add, without reference at the moment to books or memoranda. But cure in even one case out of every four, and improvement in one of every two, is no inconsiderable achievement when we remember the hard and almost hopeless material with which the Labour House has to deal, and the virtual inability of our own method of treating the vagrant and the loafer to effect any reformative result whatever. Obviously, it is impossible to expect accurate statistics on the question, for reasons not by any means confined to the impossibility of following the history of every discharged case, but one fact alone tells an eloquent tale. The Labour House for Westphalia was erected in 1821. Since that time the population of the province has vastly increased, and the economic revolution consummated in the interval has created a new kind of itinerancy, that of machine-bred labour, yet it has not been found necessary to enlarge the Labour House, whose capacity is to-day as adequate to the demands made upon it as it was ninety years ago. Not only so, but (disregarding the abnormal numbers of the last two years) the number of offenders of the kind for whom the institution exists is actually decreasing proportionately to population.

The following were the commitments to Benninghausen during the twenty years 1890 to 1909:—

	Men	Women	Total
1890	329	71	400
1891	398	64	462
1892	325	44	369
1893	361	51	412
1894	378	41	419
1895	330	45	375

1896	287	51	338
1897	272	64	336
1899	273	49	307
1899	258	53	326
1900	239	65	304
1901	312	46	358
1902	336	42	378
1903	321	57	375
1904	355	39	394
1905	360	45	405
1906	305	35	340
1907	343	24	367
1908	442	40	482
1909	445	48	493

Other causes have, no doubt, helped to bring about this relative diminution in the number of commitments—amongst them the development of the Voluntary Labour Colonies with their ever-open doors—but at Benninghausen it is believed that the operation of the anti-vagrancy law takes the first place.

Probably the question has before now passed through the reader's mind—what becomes of the 300 or 400 men and women who are returned from the

Labour House to liberty in the course of every year? When a prisoner has served his time a problem arises which requires the most circumspect handling. What shall be done with him? Shall he be simply turned adrift at the gates in the hope that he will continue to follow in freedom the path of industry which he has entered while under restraint? The Benninghausen Labour House makes no such wreck of its own reformative work. On the contrary, every effort is made to encourage the prisoner to persist in a regular and honest life. He is allowed to choose his destination, and the Police Authorities of the locality are communicated with beforehand, so that they may be ready to provide for his temporary lodging, and either to help him to work themselves or to enlist the offices of private persons able so to do. In towns there always exists some philanthropic society which is ready to take the case in hand; in the country the helping hand is often that of the clergyman, Roman Catholic or Protestant, as the case may be. Here also is seen the utility of the Labour Colony—and to Westphalia, be it noted, belongs the honour of having founded the original Colony, of which the thirty-three others scattered over Germany are copies—which frequently serves as a temporary refuge for men who, having passed through the mill of adversity and humiliation, and been given a glimpse of better things, have no desire to drift into the old demoralising ways.

CHAPTER VII.

THE BERLIN MUNICIPAL LABOUR HOUSE.

The Labour House at Rummelsburg, near Berlin, is an example of a house of correction for offenders of the classes dealt with at Benninghausen conducted by a municipality. This institution is maintained entirely by the City of Berlin, and while it exists to meet the requirements of the Imperial Penal Code, as already explained, there is attached to it a large hospital which closely corresponds to an English workhouse infirmary.

This hospital is intended for the reception of (1) persons suffering from incurable diseases, also infirm persons who are no longer able to look after themselves, even with the assistance of outrelief; (2) those, who, owing to their past irregular mode of life (intemperance, immorality, criminality, etc.), are unsuited to admission to the usual municipal infirmaries; (3) destitute persons who might still be given outrelief, but who, by reason of their irregular mode of life, as above stated, would be better provided for in a public institution; (4) those in receipt of relief who are believed to be likely to give way to mendicity; and finally (5) persons sentenced to disciplinary detention who are infirm or ill, and incapable of work. In general, the class of persons accommodated are the undeserving infirm poor who are not thought worthy of permanent association with indoor paupers of more or less respectable antecedents. Although under the management of the same Director, and administered by the same Committee of the Town Council, the hospital is entirely independent of the house of correction, and its inmates are disregarded in the statistical data which follow.

The numbers detained at Rummelsburg during the financial year 1907-8 were as follows:—

	Males.	Females.	Total
Number detained on April 1, 1908	1,349	36	1,385
Admitted during year	1,428	102	1,530
	2,777	138	2,915

Discharged during the year	1,128	55	1,183
Died	21	—	21
	1,149	55	1,204
Number remaining on March 31, 1909	1,628	83	1,711

Of the 1530 persons admitted during the year 1381 (1,282 men and 99 women) had been committed by the Police Authorities of Berlin, and 149 (146 men and 3 women) were reinstated with a view to their completing sentences interrupted owing either to temporary removal to hospital or to escape.

The offences which led to commitment were the following:—

	Males.	Females.	Total.
Vagabondage	11	—	11
Begging	655	7	662
Homelessness	567	61	628
Souteneurs	49	31	80
Totals	1,282	99	1,381

The duration of the sentences awarded was as follows:—

	Males.	Females.	Total.
Six months and under	252	42	294

From six months to two years	545	43	588
Two years	485	14	499
Totals	1,282	99	1,381

Of the 1,183 persons discharged during the year, 84 went to their own homes, 921 had no homes to go to, 113 were handed to other judicial authorities, 13 were removed to outside hospitals or lunatic asylums, and 52 were removed to the infirmary after completing their sentences.

Of the persons newly admitted, 20 were twenty-one years of age or under, 76 were between twenty-one and twenty-five years, 126 between twenty-five and thirty years, 346 between thirty and forty years, 389 between forty and fifty years, 322 between fifty and sixty years, 91 between sixty and seventy years, and 11 seventy years and upwards.

The occupations of these 1,381 persons were as follows:—

	Men.	Women.	Total
Agriculture, forestry, gardening, hunting, fishing	—	—	—
Industry, mining, and building	541	3	544
Trade and commerce	122	3	125
Domestic service and casual labour	618	93	711
No occupation	1	—	1

or none stated

The inmates of the Berlin Labour House are employed in a variety of ways, but chiefly in the works connected with the irrigation farms belonging to the city. All the men of this class are lodged in barracks near the farms, so as to avoid walking the long distance to and fro every day. The remainder of the men are engaged in miscellaneous trades, such as tailoring, shoe making, clogging, wood-working, basket and brush making, lock-smithery, tinning, straw-plaiting, book binding, etc.; wood cutting is done by the less skilled men; and old men are put to light employments like coffee bean and feather sorting. Most of the women not engaged in domestic work are employed in sewing and washing for municipal institutions, like the hospitals, shelters for the homeless, the cattle market and abattoir, etc. The following table shows the manner in which the labour of the inmates was distributed amongst these employments, with the number of days worked, and the value of the work done, during the year 1908-9:—

Paid Work.

	Number of days of Work.	Value of Work.	
		£	s.
(1) *Outside the Labour House.*			
Agricultural work on the sewage farms during seven months of summer	128,526	2,570	10

Work for other municipal institutions	2,884¾	100	19
Work for officers of Municipal Orphanage and Shelter	90	3	3
(2) *Inside the Labour House.*			
Sewing (women)	230	6	15
Washing	7,214	1,854	13
Wood-cutting	20,894	361	18
Other inside work	3,714	129	19
Farm work	1,382	48	17
Work for officers in the workshops	5,418	135	9
Work for outside employers	7,403	20	19
Oakum-picking	1,900	3	11

179,655¾   5,236   13

Unpaid Work.

	Number of Days.
(1) Agricultural work on these wage farms, in five winter months (November to March)	102,968
(2) Work at the Municipal Shelter	610
(3) Artisans' work for the Labour House	34,238
(4) Gardeners' work for the Labour House	3,170
(5) Work in the kitchens	13,179
(6) Sempstresses	12,213
(7) Washing	14,428
(8) Bookbinding, writing and work of porters, stokers, etc.	44,859
(9) Cooking and other domestic work done at the sewage farms, etc.	25,544

251,209

The work of the kinds classified under Nos. 3 to 9 was charged in the books at 58 pfennige (about 7d.) per day, representing an aggregate value of £4,281 5s., making the entire imputed earnings of the inmates £9,517 8s. This amount does not include the wages or bonus paid to the inmates, as stated below.

The work-day consists of ten hours, and the time-table for week days and for Sundays and festivals is as follows:—

Weekdays.

Rise	5.45	a.m.			
First breakfast	6.0	"			
Work	6.15	"	to	9.0	a.m.
Second breakfast	9.0	"	to	9.30	"
Work	9.30	"	to	12.0	noon
Dinner, and rest	12.0	noon	to	1.30	p.m.
Work	1.30	p.m.	to	5.0	"
Work	1.30	p.m.	to	5.0	"
Supper	5.0	"	to	5.30	"
Work	5.30	"	to	6.45	"
Rest		till bedtime.			
Bedtime, and	7.0 p.m.				

lights
out

On Saturdays and the evenings before festivals work ceases at 4.0 p.m., but the intervening time until 5.45 is given to cleaning the washplaces, etc., and bedtime is 6.0 o'clock.

Sundays and Festivals.

	Summer.					Winter.			
Rise		5.45 a.m.					6.45 a.m.		
Breakfast	6.0.	a.m.	to	6.15.	a.m.	7.0.	a.m.	to	7.15. a.m.
Exercise in open air	6.15.	"	to	8.30.	"	7.15.	"	to	8.30. "
Divine service	8.30.	"	to	9.30.	"	8.30.	"	to	9.30. "
Exercise in open air	9.30.	"	to	12.0.	"	9.30.	"	to	12.0. "
Dinner	12.0.	p.m.	to	12.30.	p.m.	12.0.	p.m.	to	12.30. p.m.
Exercise in open air and relaxation	12.30	"	to	12.30.	"	12.30.	"	to	5.0. "
Supper	5.0	"	to	5.30.	"	5.0.	"	to	5.30. "
Rest	5.30	"	to	5.45.	"	5.30.	"	to	5.450. "
Bedtime		5.45 p.m.				5.45 p.m.			

While, as a rule, the hours of work are the same for all, the tasks allotted are, as far as possible, proportioned to individual capacity. One of the rules[64] of the establishment states:—

> "Every inmate is required to perform, without demur and to the best of his ability, the work allotted to him, either inside or outside the establishment. As a rule, all inmates have to work on week-days an equal number of hours, and to perform in that time a task proportionate to their capacity, the completion of which, however, does not exempt them from working to the end of the usual time. The administration may, however, under certain circumstances curtail the duration of the daily hours of work and the extent of the task in individual cases. Anyone who, owing to idleness or negligence, fails to perform his allotted task, or who in general works slothfully or negligently, will be punished. No inmate may, without permission, allow his work to be done for him by another, or do another's work."

For the encouragement of diligence and good conduct a small wage is paid. This amounts to 10 pfennige or 1½d. per day for most work, but only half this sum in the case of certain inferior occupations. The rule on the subject says:—

> "The proceeds of the work done by the inmates, on the order of the Administration, belong to the Municipality of Berlin, and are paid into the treasury of the establishment. The extra pay credited to the inmates by employers is divided into two equal parts, of which one is placed at the inmate's disposal for the purchase of extra food, the payment of postage, and other necessary expenses, during his detention, while the other accumulates as savings until his discharge."

At the beginning of the financial year 1908-9 the bonus account of the various inmates stood at £1,196 10s.; there was added during the year £2,331, and paid out £2,109 10s., leaving a balance to the credit of the inmates of £1,418. The disbursements from this account during the year included £1,249 paid to discharged inmates, £573 paid to detainees for the purchase of extras, £159 paid for clothing needed by departing inmates, and £102 charged for damage done through malice or negligence.

The utmost endeavour is made, by firm yet just treatment, to encourage the inmates in the habit of industry; the individuality and aptitude of each man are carefully studied, with a view to his employment in the manner most likely to draw out the best in him; the diligent and trustworthy are selected for the more responsible posts, and all are made to feel that their re-making lies in their own hands. Great stress is laid upon the moral basis of work, without undue obtrusion of the religious motive. One of the regulations runs:—

> "The inmates shall live together in peace and quiet, none interrupting another in his work, but rather by industry, order, and decent moral behaviour encouraging each other to reformation of life, and setting each other a good example. Conversation upon past misdemeanours may under no circumstances take place; nor may one inmate reproach another with any crime which he may have committed, or with his past mode of life."

The time allowed for leisure and relaxation cannot be called excessive, but such as it is the inmates are encouraged to employ it in reading. Special prominence is given, indeed, to the library, of which the last annual report says:—

> "The library is intended to serve the purpose which the administration of the Labour House seeks to achieve, viz., the transformation of the detainees committed to its charge into useful members of society. The educational influence of the use of books should not be depreciated. The administration earnestly endeavours, by offering to the inmates books of an entertaining, instructive and edifying character, and such as may lift them out of their everyday surroundings, and by studying the individuality and educational standard of each person, to offer them healthy stimulus during the hours of leisure. These books and the Sunday magazines which are regularly distributed are read with eagerness. The library is open to all inmates without exception."

The fact may be added that no less than £25 a year is spent on the provision of new books. As for other moral influences, religious services are held regularly on Sundays and festivals, and Holy Communion is administered at intervals, for Protestant and Roman Catholic detainees separately.

Little fault is found with the general conduct of the inmates, in spite of the fact that the majority are old offenders. The character of the material with which the Labour House has to deal may be judged from the following summary of the punishments which had been undergone by those newly admitted in the year 1908-9:—

Mode of Punishment	Men.	Women.	Total.
Labour House (house of correction)	791	50	841
Labour House more than three times	558	13	571
Close detention more than ten times	371	22	393
Close detention more than twenty times	538	33	571
Prison	916	59	975
Gaol	127	3	130
Imprisoned before eighteenth year	23	—	23

Nevertheless, during the year punishments for offenders against discipline were awarded to only 304 inmates in 352 cases. The percentage of the male inmates punished (calculated on the mean daily average detained) was twenty-one, and of the female inmates 12. The punishments begin with mere reproof, and then follow in order of severity: withdrawal of permission to receive visits for a time, withdrawal of permission to write or receive letters, forfeit of the right to supplement the Labour House diet out of the reward of industry, forfeit of earnings themselves, disallowal of open air exercise, curtailment of rations, simple cell detention, and finally imprisonment on hard fare. Only in case of violent insubordination may chains or the straight jacket be resorted to.

It is difficult to speak definitely as to the permanent influence upon these people of Labour House treatment. The proportion who leave the House "reformed" in the usual acceptance of the word is, no doubt, small, as the large percentage of re-committals proves. Viewing the institution less from the individual than the social standpoint, however, the fact remains that under restraint the average loafer shows that he is able to work, and to work well. Not only so, but the cost of his detention is not excessive. During the year to which all the foregoing figures relate, the entire cost of maintenance and administration, both of the Labour House and the Hospital, including interest at 3½ per cent. upon the value of the land and buildings, was £55,101, or deducting £5,236 received for work done by the inmates (exclusive of that done for the establishment), £49,865, equal to 1s. 3d. per head per day for the whole of the inmates. The cost of able-bodied inmates only was estimated at a fraction under 11d. per head per day, or 6s. 3d. per week.

Tables are added showing the average number of inmates in the Labour House during the years 1899 to 1908, and the commitments for begging only during nineteen years:—

Average Number of Inmates (all Classes).

	Males.	Females.	Total.
1899	1,080	124	1,204
1900	1,107	151	1,258
1901	1,128	150	1,278
1902	1,600	152	1,752
1903	1,660	117	1,777
1904	1,694	145	1,839
1905	1,849	129	1,978

1906	1,685	117	1,802
1907	1,369	65	1,434
1908	1,403	58	1,461

Commitments for Begging.

1889-1890	709
1890-1891	656
1891-1892	916
1892-1893	1,253
1894	1,087
1895	925
1896	824
1897	715
1898	633
1899	735
1900	641
1901	868
1902	984

1903	1,053
1904	1,008
1905	823
1906	587
1907	594
1908	662

It should be pointed out, however, that the latter figures afford no indication whatever as to the frequency of the offence of mendicancy in Berlin. Detention in the Labour House is a secondary punishment, and those who receive it form only a small proportion of the total number of persons prosecuted for begging. The following statement shows, for a period of twelve years, the numbers apprehended, prosecuted, and convicted in Berlin for this offence (the difference between the apprehensions and prosecutions represents those who were simply warned and discharged):—

Year.	Apprehensions.	Prosecutions.	Convictions.
1894	21,678	19,244	11,216
1895	19,318	16,780	9,434
1896	22,048	19,064	10,058
1897	23,434	20,343	10,681
1898	20,378	16,931	8,781
1899	16,556	13,672	7,043
1900	17,334	14,097	7,246
1901	17,334	14,097	7,246

1902	23,582	18,962	11,545
1903	21,576	17,524	10,706
1904	19,019	15,562	10,069
1905	16,148	13,197	8,301

Comparing the average number of apprehensions for mendicancy during the last five years with those of the first five in the table, a decrease will be found of from 21,371 to 20,199, in spite of a large increase in the population.

CHAPTER VIII.

THE TREATMENT OF VAGRANCY IN SWITZERLAND.

It is a noteworthy fact that the treatment of the vagrant and the loafer on disciplinary principles has been carried out most systematically in countries so fundamentally different in political government as Germany and Switzerland. In the Swiss Republic this question is regulated by Cantonal laws. The Federal Legislation on the subject, dating from 1850, merely orders that vagrants and mendicants shall be dealt with in the cantons in which they may be arrested in accordance with the laws of those cantons, yet adding that, if of foreign nationality, they shall be expelled from the country.

While, therefore, each canton makes its own vagrancy laws, the spirit of these laws is entirely free from the weak sentimentality which, in some respects, characterises our own. The law in force in the canton of Berne, for example, states that:

> "Vagrancy, namely, the wandering from place to place of persons without means and without the object of obtaining honest employment, is punishable with imprisonment and hard labour not exceeding sixty days, or with committal to a labour institution for a term between six months and two years; on the repetition of the offence the vagrant is always to be committed to a labour institution."

Persons who apply for help from a Relief Station and refuse to accept suitable work when offered to them may be treated as "shirkers" (work-shy), and as such they are liable to detention in a labour institution for any period between several months and several years. The police are empowered to arrest beggars without special warrant, and the husbands and fathers who evade their domestic responsibilities, and even the town loafer who hangs about at street corners, may be apprehended and committed to a Forced Labour House by very summary process. These institutions are cantonal, and one of the best is that at Witzwil, established in 1895 by the Canton of Berne, and conducted by the Cantonal Police Authority.

The offenders detained at Witzwil are of five classes:—

(1) First offenders convicted of criminal offences or sentenced to a house of correction in the Canton of Berne, where the sentence does not exceed three years. Those likely to abscond, or belonging to other Cantons, are not accepted.

(2) Offenders sentenced to simple detention.

(3) Bernese offenders sentenced by Military Courts to a gaol or convict prison for not more than three years.

(4) Persons sentenced to a Labour House by legal process.

(5) Persons belonging to other Cantons.

The minimum term of detention is two months, the maximum five years, but one-third of the sentence may be remitted as a reward of good conduct.

A twenty years' contract exists between the Cantons of Berne and Neuchâtel under which the latter Canton is empowered on terms to send to Witzwil harmless prisoners whose sentences exceed two months. Some prisoners are also received from the Canton of Geneva. The arrangement is attended by certain disadvantages for Berne, but these are over-ruled by financial considerations.

The Witzwil Forced Labour Colony is situated between the lakes of Neuchâtel, Biel, and Murten, upon a tract of land known as the Great Moss, which has for centuries been subject to frequent inundations from the Aare and many smaller streams, but which, at the expense of the adjacent Cantons of Berne, Freiburg, Vaud, and Neuchâtel, assisted by the Federal Government, was, many years ago, brought into cultivable condition by diverting the main streams, and carrying out extensive drainage works.

The estate comprises about 2,000 acres, the larger part of which was bought, as marsh-land, from the adjacent communes some forty years ago by an Agricultural Co-operative Society for the purpose of development. On the failure of this Society the Canton of Berne became the owner in 1891 at a cost of about £30,000 for land and buildings, the latter then in bad condition. The communications are good, since there are two railway stations within two miles of the centre of the estate. The land is, on the whole, fertile when properly drained, and a portion of it is of excellent quality and suitable for winter wheat, clover, and grass; other portions are more suited to pasture, vegetables, and forestry, and there is a stretch of peat land and sand.

When the estate was adopted for the purpose of a Forced Labour Colony the first works carried out on a large scale were road making, drainage, and building, and these have greatly increased the value of the Colony. There are two distinct farms, Lindenhof and Nusshof, the latter being now used as a Voluntary Labour Colony for discharged prisoners. The Lindenhof Colony is the principal one, and the buildings there comprise (1) the administrative block; (2) a large prison, containing 100 habitable cells, punishment cells, school, church, sickroom, kitchen, offices, workrooms for tailors, shoemakers, saddlers, basket makers, and book binders, with other workrooms in which the prisoners can be employed in straw work, besom making, etc., in bad weather; also living and bedrooms for the attendants, out-buildings and cellars; (3) dwelling-house, with bakery, washhouse, laundry, and bedrooms for officers and attendants; (4) workshops for workers in iron and wood, with rooms for the necessary machines; (5) stalls and sheds for 270 cattle, 30 horses, and 150 pigs, hay and straw lofts, and dwellings for the farm servants and their families; (6) machine room and warehouses.

The buildings belonging to the Nusshof Colony comprise (1) two dwelling houses for the superintendent and his family and the assistants, quarters for discharged prisoners who have returned to Witzwil owing to their being without employment, and who receive food, lodging, and a small money payment in return for their labour; (2) stalls and sheds for 100 cows, several oxen, hay and straw lofts and cellars for root crops. The other buildings scattered about the estate include a cheesery, dwellings for hinds and their families and for turbary labourers, cattle-sheds, barns, and peat sheds, etc. There is an electric power and light station, and the principal depots are connected by telephone.

For some years all necessary buildings, roads, drainage, etc., have been done by the prisoners under the direction of paid overseers, and in this way the value of the estate has been greatly increased.

The number of prisoners varies from 110 to 150. As a rule, from two to five prisoners escape yearly (attempts not counted), but the majority of them are recaptured. Violent and exceptionally contumacious prisoners and those likely to escape are transferred to the convict prison at Thorberg.

The principles on which the prisoners are employed are defined as follows:—

(1) Work should, as far as possible, conform to the prisoners capacity and enable him on his discharge to earn his livelihood more easily.

(2) Prison work should be productive ("create actual values"), should entail muscular exertion yet not be injurious to health, and should yield as high a return as possible without injuring free labour.

(3) The work should be so arranged as to further the educative purpose of punishment.

The newly arrived prisoner soon falls into his place. He is at once dressed in the prison uniform and handed over to an overseer, who questions him as to his past occupation and capacity, and he is then assigned to a gang, as a unit of which he begins regular work the following morning. The prisoners' labour is divided between farm work of various kinds, works of reclamation, peat cutting, fruit and vegetable culture, forestry, and handicrafts. The men engaged on the land work in gangs of ten or twelve, each under the control of two unarmed officers. As to the latter it is said that great stress is laid on the importance of their not merely supervising the men, but taking active part in the work, so as to stimulate them by example, and also to get acquainted with them. The day's routine in summer is as follows:—5.30 (6.0 in winter) to 9.0, work; 9.0 to 9.20, interval for a light meal; 9.20 to 11.30 work; 11.30 to 12.30, dinner and rest; 12.30 to 4.0, work; 4.0 to 4.20, interval for a light meal; 4.20 to 7.0, work, followed by supper, house work, and bed. In winter the dark hours of work are spent in the barns or workshops, as may be expedient. The principal occupations in the latter are tailoring, shoe making, smithery, and carpentering, and most of the work done is for the institution. The men sleep, eat, and spend their spare time in separate cells, for intercourse between them is strictly discouraged.

Although no claim to payment is recognised a certain sum, not exceeding 2 francs (1s. 6d.) per month, is credited to every man's account, and the aggregate is paid out to him on discharge; his clothes are then thoroughly repaired or new ones are given to him, and his railway fare is paid, as far as the Swiss frontier, if necessary; in case of need relief is also given to a prisoner's dependents during his incarceration.

The dietary is as follows:—Morning, coffee with milk, potatoes and bread; noon, soup, with vegetables or flour, with meat and salad twice a week; evening, soup and fresh fruit (the latter being occasionally given with Sunday dinner as well). The daily ration of bread is from 22 to 27 ounces, while soup, coffee and vegetables are served to every man *ad libitum*.

The moral interests of the prisoners are not overlooked. There is a school for the benefit of such young men as choose to attend; every Saturday books and magazines of an edifying and entertaining character are distributed for use the following day; concerts and lectures are given from time to time; and the religious needs of the Colony are ministered to by two visiting chaplains. Letter-writing and visits of friends are allowed once a month.

The number of prisoners on January 1, 1908, was 156, 279 were admitted and 237 were discharged (including 2 deaths and 2 escapes) during the year, and there remained on December 31, 198. The maximum number detained was 198, and the minimum 154. Of the 279 new prisoners 204 were detained for the first time. Further, 172 were single men, 76 were married, 15 were widowers, and 16 were separated from their wives. As to occupations 107 were agricultural labourers, factory operatives, and general labourers, and the remainder represented more than thirty trades. There were 31 foreigners amongst the new prisoners (13 per cent. of the whole), 13 being Italians, 9 Germans, and 6 French. Of the sentences, 148 were for less than six months, 68 were for six and under twelve months, 51 were for one year and under two years, and 12 were for two years and over.

The total number of days worked during the year was 50,531, divided as follows:—

Small earnings	1,525
Domestic service and cooking	1,660
Washing	612
Baking	332
Tailoring	1,332
Shoemaking and saddlery	1,084
Wood working	1,177
Iron working	1,614
Basket-plaiting	279
Turf cutting	782
Building works	3,723
General labour	535
Improvement works	2,587
Agriculture	33,309
Total	33,309

To look after and direct the work of this body of men 48 officers and employees of all kinds were necessary, comprising 3 general overseers, 1 machinist, 28 foremen and chief stockmen in the agricultural departments, 1 saddler, 1 tailor, 1 shoemaker, 1 wheelwright, 1 carpenter, 1 smith, 1 mason (the last seven being skilled men), 3 office employees, and 6 domestic servants.

The revenue in 1908 was £5,567, of which £4,602 was derived from the various departments of the farm, £740 from the workshops, and £225 from boarding fees paid by public authorities. The expenditure was £5,647, of which £1,041 fell to administrative costs, £3,997 to food and maintenance, and £445 to rent. It does not appear that interest on the original outlay is allowed for, but, on the other hand, a very considerable addition is made yearly to the value of the estate owing to the improvement works which are carried out.

The punishments awarded for offences against discipline during 1908 numbered 53, *viz.*, 16 men were imprisoned for one night in the punishment cells for quarrelsomeness, disturbance, and laziness; 29 had one or two days' cell imprisonment for disobedience and contumacy, and 8 had from two to eight days' cell imprisonment for absconding, attempts at the same, and smuggling. "Our general impression of the discipline preserved in the past year," the Director reports, "is not unfavourable; more than one case of punishment might have been avoided if the overseers had always understood their duty better, and if their insubordinates had shown a better spirit, but when one remembers how keenly many of our inmates chafe against the loss of their liberty it is not surprising if now and then one loses control over himself. It is often difficult for the foreigners—especially the French—to obey orders, and with the exception of a Genevan, all the prisoners who tried to escape were foreigners."

Every endeavour is made to obtain settled work for discharged prisoners, but some are retained for a time as paid labourers, and others are taken in at the Nusshof branch of the Colony.

Nusshof is governed by separate regulations, which run as follows:—

> "(1) The Administration of Witzwil has established at Nusshof a home for discharged prisoners, for the purpose of offering to such of them as desire to make a sensible use of their regained freedom, residence for a longer or shorter time by way of transition.
>
> "(2) Engagement is by means of contract, which must be signed both by the colonist and the overseer of Nusshof.
>
> "(3) The colonists are required so to conduct themselves as to give occasion to no complaints.
>
> "(4) The colonists are required to observe the regulation in all particulars. Breaches of the same, such as drunkenness

and disorderly behaviour, entail instant dismissal, to which the overseer may resort on his own responsibility.

"(5) The colonists may not leave the Witzwil estate without the permission of the Administration.

"(6) Colonists who show diligence and ability may find permanent employment in positions of responsibility.

"(7) The colonists receive free board and lodging, and in addition working clothes. Special contracts are concluded with artisans ensuring payment in money.

"(8) Colonists who enter in winter (*i.e.*, between November 15 and the end of February) receive for this time no money payment. Those, on the other hand, who enter in summer and autumn (*i.e.*, between March 1 and the end of October), and work to the satisfaction of the Administration, receive in winter also a reduced money payment to be fixed by the overseer.

"(9) The money payment ranges from 50 centimes to 1.50 franc (5d. to 1s. 3d.) per day. The overseer fixes the commencing wage.

"(10) During the period of the contract the Administration decides the amount of the money payment. Part of the wages shall be used for the provision of clothing and linen; the balance, if not necessary for the support of members of the colonist's family, is put away as savings. The Administration or the colonist's employer fixes the date at which the amount due to a colonist, together with his savings bank-book, shall be paid to him."

In 1908 the colonists at Nusshof numbered 62, and they worked 4,136 days, representing an average stay, including Sundays, of about eleven weeks, while money wages of £115 in the aggregate were paid to them.

Another Swiss Forced Labour Colony is that of St. Johannsen, near the lake of Bienne, established in 1884 by the Canton of Berne "for the improvement of disorderly and work-shy adults," and likewise administered by the Cantonal Police. It can accommodate 180 persons, but the usual complement is about 160. The area of the farm is some 400 acres, and the land is very similar to that at Witzwil, and has been reclaimed in the same manner. Here, too, farm work and simple trades—shoe making, carpentering, basket making, and smithery—are carried on side by side, and the general conditions of life, the length of the sentences, the prospects of remission, and the results are much the same in the two Colonies. Work is severe at St. Johannsen, and under the discipline some of the younger men are said to shed their idle habits, but little impression seems to be made upon the older ones.

A third Forced Labour Colony, at Gmünden, near St. Gall, serves the Canton of Appenzell, and was established in 1884, and its principal inmates are "able-bodied men, who from irregular or dissolute life, or work-shyness become a charge on the district, who require special supervision, who neglect their families, or who are guilty of disorderly conduct in the poor-houses"—such people being committed by the District Council, "in order to accustom them to hard work and regular life"—while others are police law offenders who have failed to pay fines imposed upon them by the magistrates. The estate consists of 100 acres, and the accommodation is for fifty inmates, but the average number is thirty-five. The principal economy of the farm is arboriculture, but part of the land is used as a dairy farm, and the trades of shoe-making, carpentering, and weaving are also followed. The average term of detention is a year in the case of the loafer, and three months in the case of the Police Court defaulters, but by good conduct a man may earn a partial remission of his sentence. As at Witzwil the officers are not armed, but there is no complaint of violence. Work is found for many of the men on leaving, and they often carry away with them a sum of money, the proceeds of a bonus on good work, which helps to give them a new start. The District Council pays £4 per annum for each person whom it commits, and by the aid of this charge and the proceeds of the men's labour the Colony is able to show a profit.

The Canton of Basle-Rural has a similar Colony at Liesthal, between Basle and Olten, recruited from the same classes of offenders as those at Gmünden. Only about seventy men can be received here, and special attention is given to plain industrial work, only the older colonists engaging in farm work. The District Councils commit to the Colony mendicants, loafers, habitual drunkards, and men who neglect to maintain their families, and pay between £2 and £3 annually per head for their support, but the Colony is far from being self-supporting.

It is maintained that mendicity has greatly decreased in Switzerland during recent years, and all who know the country will agree that, save in districts which are overrun by foreign visitors—yet not in all these—the beggar and the loafer are comparatively uncommon. Nevertheless, it would be wrong to attribute this immunity entirely to the existence of Forced Labour Houses and Colonies, though these have, no doubt, helped. It must be remembered that Switzerland has an excellent system of Relief Stations for wayfarers, and has of late years taken up the Voluntary Labour Colony movement with much zeal.[65] Further, the Swiss workman is far less restive than his colleague in Germany, for example, and the spirit of local patriotism tends to keep him in his native canton and often in his native commune, however small and sequestered it may be. Finally, the Swiss are probably the hardest working, as they are certainly the hardiest, people in Europe, and they deem voluntary idleness to be one of the most disreputable and culpable of social offences.

CHAPTER IX.

LABOUR HOUSES UNDER THE POOR LAW.

The practice of confining in forced labour institutions persons who, in various ways, have become defaulters under the Poor Law, particularly by neglecting to maintain dependents for whose support they are legally responsible, is no new one; both in Germany and Switzerland Labour Houses of this kind have existed for many years. The German Imperial Penal Code, as we have seen, provides for the commitment to Labour Houses of those who "give way to gambling, intemperance, and idleness" so that they are compelled to seek public relief, either for themselves, or those dependent upon them. Prior to the passing of this law Poor Law Authorities in some of the States were already empowered to put such persons to forced labour. As a result of the Imperial enactment, Prussia repealed its law on the subject (dated May 21, 1855), but Saxony, Wurtemberg, Oldenburg and Mecklenburg Schwerin retained their legislation, and within the last six years Anhalt and the Free City of Hamburg have adopted laws to the same effect.

Before speaking in detail of a typical Poor Law Labour House of this kind, it may be well to summarise the provisions of the principal laws on the subject.

The Poor-relief Ordinance of Saxony, dated October 22, 1840, states that the power to compel persons who are "work-shy" to labour belongs to the jurisdiction of the Police Authority, with which the Poor Law Authority, when independent of the former Authority, has to agree upon the necessary measures. As a result of this Ordinance the rural Poor Law unions have established district Labour Houses under the administration of the local governors, while some of the larger towns have established institutions of their own, managed subject to regulations approved by the Government.

Persons are committed to these Labour Houses both by the Poor Law and Police Authorities, the term of detention being indefinite, but if a man who has been committed on account of neglect of family is able to show that he has provided a home for his dependents, he can require to be discharged.

The existing law of Wurtemberg (July 2, 1889) empowers Poor Law Authorities to put to forced labour any man whose wife or children under fourteen years receive public relief; it is not necessary that he should himself have applied for such relief to be granted. The laws of Anhalt (April 27, 1904) and Mecklenburg Schwerin (1871 and 1890) are to the same effect.

By the law of Oldenburg (March 14, 1870) the following persons may be committed to the Forced Labour House of Vechta: Drunkards, persons who abuse the poor relief granted to them, women who, having had two or more illegitimate children for whom they have had to seek relief, again become *enceinte*, and (by Ministerial Decree of April 25, 1888) parents who neglect their children so that they fall upon the Poor Law. For a first commitment the period of detention is two years, for repetitions three years.

The latest provisions of the kind are those which were embodied in the amended Poor Law of Hamburg in 1907. Section 21 of this law states:—

> "Any person who receives public relief, either for himself or for those dependent upon him, may be required by resolution of the Poor Law Labour Committee, in so far as may be requisite in order to remove or diminish existing destitution, to perform work suited to his capacity. In the event of refusal to do the work assigned to him by the Committee, the decision of that body may be put in operation by direct force. In the end the person relieved may be placed in a Labour House against his will. These provisions do not apply to cases of destitution caused by transient circumstances."

This compulsion may be applied even when the defaulters dependents are maintained without his consent or against his will.

The Committee which exercises these powers consists of five members—a member (a Senator) of the Poor Law Board, as president, two members of that Board elected by the House of Burgesses, and two chairmen of Poor Law districts or almoners. A decision to commit a Poor Law defaulter to the Labour House must be supported by a majority of four votes to one, and appeal is allowed both to the Senate and the ordinary Courts of Law, but a decision remains in operation unless and until quashed. The alleged defaulter is entitled to appear, and to be represented, at the proceedings of the Committee. A person against whom an order of detention has been put in operation can at any time ask for its repeal, but the Committee is only obliged to reconsider its decision after three months have passed; when a year has elapsed, however, the detainee must be released for a period of at least six months in order to test his willingness to meet his obligations.

The reason advanced for the amendment of the law was that the number of wife deserters had for a long time been on the increase, and that existing measures had proved ineffectual.

There has been a good deal of controversy upon the question whether the enactment of forced labour for Poor Law defaulters conflicts with Section 361, paras. 5, 7, and 10, and Section 362 of the Imperial Penal Code, but the judgment of the Imperial Department of Justice is in the negative, provided that such labour be required by way of restitution of relief afforded, and not as a punishment for misdemeanour, and that no definite term of detention be imposed. Institutions established for the reception of such persons, therefore, must be regarded as reformative in character, and not in any formal sense as penal.

It is unlikely that a British Legislature would be willing to depute to Poor Law Authorities, even of the reformed type proposed by the Poor Law Commission, power to put to forced labour defaulters of the kind referred to. Nor does it accord with our national ideas of justice that the same authority—in this case a civil body—should be able to act simultaneously as plaintiff and judge. The Legislature of the State of Hamburg entertained scruples upon both these points, and for that reason, besides allowing an offender to answer a proposal of committal, both in person and by legal adviser, it devised a double form of appeal. In this country the only practicable form of procedure would be by magisterial order, as at present, except that defaulters would, on conviction, be committed to a Labour House for disciplinary treatment, instead of as now to prison.

Among the German towns in which Poor Law Authorities possess and enforce the powers here referred to, are the four Saxon towns of Dresden, Leipzig, Chemnitz, and Plauen, also Stuttgart, Hamburg, Oldenburg, Ulm, Heilbronn, Ludwigsburg, Rostock, Schwerin, and Dessau. I have described the Dresden Labour House in another place,[66] and it will be sufficient for present purposes to summarise the principal characteristics of the Leipzig institution.

MUNICIPAL LABOUR HOUSE AT LEIPZIG.

This municipal Labour House is one of the oldest institutions of the town, for the building was anciently a monastic hospital; later it served for the reception of orphans, deserted and neglected children, imbeciles, etc., and it has been applied to its present purpose for some seventeen years.

The Labour House is officially described as serving for "the detention, suitable employment, and moral improvement" of the following classes of people:—

(*a*) Work-shy, intemperate and dissolute persons who, owing to their mode of life, become chargeable, or cause others for whose maintenance they are responsible to become chargeable, to the Poor Law.

(*b*) Persons under eighteen years who become a public nuisance owing to demoralisation, neglect, or idleness, and whose detention is proposed by their parents or guardians.

(*c*) Children under fifteen years who are in danger of moral contamination until they can be placed in reformatories, in so far as it is inexpedient to admit them into the Municipal Orphanage.

(*d*) Homeless persons whom it is inexpedient to place elsewhere (in this case only temporary detention is contemplated).

(*e*) Persons sentenced by the police to simple detention with hard labour.

(*f*) Persons sentenced by the Police to simple detention who wish to be employed during their term of confinement and who voluntarily enter the House.

It may be observed in passing that the regulations of the Dresden Labour House provide for the commitment thereto of fathers who neglect to provide for their illegitimate children, and that though the regulations of the Leipzig Labour House are silent upon the point, the Poor Law Board there likewise commits such defaulters.

Persons belonging to the first four classes enumerated above are committed by decision of the Poor Law Board, those belonging to the fourth class by the Police Authority as well, and those belonging to the fifth and sixth classes by the latter authority exclusively. Loafers and disorderly persons (*a*) and (*b*) are committed in the first instance for an indefinite period; "their detention in the institution (runs the regulation), shall, as a rule, last until the principal purpose of their committal, which is their improvement—*i.e.*, to accustom them to work, to keep them to an orderly and regulated mode of life, and to train them or make them willing to observe the duty of maintaining the members of their families—appears to have been achieved." Whether this object has been attained or not is judged by the life and habits of the detainee on discharge. Contrary to the principle acted upon at Merxplas, "the mere proof that the detainee is able to find work outside the Labour House does not justify a claim to release." Before any person is discharged the Poor Law Board considers a report made by the Director of the Labour House, and this body previously determines the period during which the conduct of an inmate is to be specially watched with a view to weighing his fitness for release. As a rule a report is required as to the conduct of every detainee a month after committal and it must be made at the latest a year after. The Board may decide to give a person liberty for any period up to six months on trial, reserving the right to require him to report himself in the interval and to detain him again should his record be unsatisfactory.

The Labour House has departments for males and for females, in every respect entirely dissociated, and in each department persons under eighteen years are forbidden contact with adults.

All persons detained whose physical condition allows of it, are put to work within the institution suited in kind and degree to their capacity, but subject to conditions work outside may also be allotted to them. The general rule is eleven and a half hours of work daily (Sundays and festivals excluded) in summer, and ten and a half hours in winter, but the Director fixes the actual task to be done in every individual case according to his discretion. The regulations state:—

> "It is the object of the labour tasks to accustom those detained to regular work, so that on their discharge they may be in a position to earn their livelihood independently in an honest way, and again to live a regular life; at the same time, an endeavour shall be made to use their labour in such a way as shall be most advantageous for the institution."

The occupations followed by men include, in addition to work in the establishment, gardening, building, joinery, shoemaking, tailoring, bookbinding, lock-smithery, painting and varnishing, wood cutting, coffee sorting, horsehair pulling, and the making of mats, besoms, paper bags, cigar holders, umbrella sticks, boxes, etc. The women are principally employed in domestic and laundry work, sewing and knitting, tobacco packing, and coffee sorting.

The hours of work are as follows: Summer, 6.0 a.m. to 12.0 noon and 1.0 to 7.0 p.m.; winter, 7.0 a.m. to 12.0 noon and 1.0 to 7.0 p.m.; with intervals of a quarter of an hour at 9.45 a.m. and 4.0 p.m.; but those who work within closed rooms are allowed, in addition, half an hour's exercise in the open air daily. The utmost diligence is required during work; no talking is allowed; and smoking and tobacco chewing are resolutely forbidden at all times, though snuff-taking is allowed "by special favour." As a reward for "specially good behaviour" certain privileges are granted in the matter of food.

While the proceeds of the inmates' labour are claimed by the institution, those who do more than their allotted tasks are credited with money allowances to the maximum of one-fifth of the total value of their work, as calculated at a given rate; and this money (less damage to tools, etc.) may be spent in the purchase of extras, in the support of dependents, etc., the balance, if any, being paid to the creditor on discharge, in one sum or in instalments, either direct or through a third person.

Insubordination and other offences are not infrequent, and there is a long gradation of punishments, beginning with formal reproof, either alone or in presence of other detainees, and rising by many steps to cell imprisonment for twelve hours in a cage which allows only of standing and sitting, and finally to corporal punishment, a punishment which has practically fallen into desuetude and which in no case is awarded to women or men over sixty years. The majority of offences are of a minor character and are punished by some curtailment of diet.

Counting only the persons who were committed or admitted to the Labour House for reformative reasons, the number dealt with in 1908 was 721; 250 (200 men and 50 women) being in confinement at the beginning of the year, and 471 being newly admitted. The maximum number was 338, and was recorded in February; the minimum was 180, recorded in July; and the daily mean for the year was 253.

The Labour House received in addition, however, a large number of persons who had been sentenced by the police to simple detention with or without labour (Classes *e* and *f*), and a large shelter connected with it lodged 12,655 persons for an aggregate of 36,413 times; of these persons, 634 were proved to be vagabonds and loafers, and the remaining 12,021 were artisans and labourers without employment.

The reasons for compulsory or voluntary detention in that year were as follows:—

	Males.	Females.	Total
(1) Destitution by reason of idleness, drunkenness, or irregular life:—			
(*a*) Personal destitution	22	6	28
(*b*) Destitution of dependants	90	17	107
(2) Demoralised persons	19	26	45

under 18 years			
(2) Demoralised persons under 18 years	19	26	45
(3) Children detained for observation prior to transfer to a reformatory	3	1	4
(4) Temporarily detained by reason of homelessness	283	4	287
Total	417	54	471
Committed on compulsion	204	50	254
Entered voluntarily	213	4	217

The detainees discharged during the year numbered 421 and were classified as follows:—

	Males.	Females.	Total
Discharged or out on parole	275	24	299

Removed to hospital, poorhouse, lunatic asylum, and orphanage correctional institutions	28	8	36
Removal to penal or correctional institutions	19	6	25
Absconded	53	7	60
Deaths	1	—	1
Totals	376	45	421

The terms of their detention were as follows:—

	Men.	Women.	Total.	Per Cent.
6 weeks or under	66	10	76	18.0
6 weeks to 3 months	75	9	84	20.0
3 months to 6 months	131	19	150	35.6

6 months to 9 months	79	6	85	20.2
9 months to 12 months	19	—	19	4.5
Over 12 months	6	1	7	1.7
Total	376	45	421	100.0

During 1908 the inmates performed 65,091½ days of work, the value of which was £3,474; of this sum, £184 was paid to them in wages, so that the net proceeds of their labour amounted to 1s. for every day worked by the inmates. The cost of maintenance (deducting revenue) averaged, during the five years 1903 to 1907, nearly 1s. 5d. per head per day, and the cost of food only 5½d. The institution derives an income of about £1,600 from endowments, and the actual cost to the municipal funds during those years was under 6d. per head per day.

It may be interesting to add a statement showing the admissions to the correctional department of the Labour House for a series of years. It will be seen that while there have been fluctuations, no absolute increase is shown.

Year.	Males.		Females.		Total.
	On compulsion.	Voluntarily.	On compulsion.	Voluntarily.	
1892	64	111	8	16	199
1893	228	195	25	31	479
1894	194	182	31	31	442

1895	160	227	23	46	456
1896	161	167	19	34	381
1897	200	93	23	26	342
1898	185	154	23	19	381
1899	109	252	7	25	393
1900	70	245	13	22	350
1901	88	313	13	18	432
1902	80	276	16	16	388
1903	76	261	22	10	369
1904	91	241	29	11	372
1905	109	238	37	5	389
1906	90	274	37	4	405
1907	77	222	22	5	326
1908	204	213	50	4	471

BERNE POORHOUSE OF KÜHLEWYL.

A Swiss example of a virtual Forced Labour Colony carried on as a part of the machinery of the Poor Law is the Kühlewyl Poorhouse belonging to the municipality of Berne. This institution was created some eighteen years ago for the reception of several distinct classes of inmates (to the exclusion of children), and principally for (1) persons permanently unable to work and support themselves, and having no means of subsistence, and (2) persons either altogether or partially unable to maintain themselves whose lodgment in such an institution seemed "justifiable in the public interest." The latter phrase is a significant one. What it implies will be best understood from a passage in a report addressed to the Municipal Council Committee, which, under the guidance of the mayor of the day, formulated the scheme. "We regard it," they said, "as of the greatest importance that there be established for Berne a Poorhouse in which all such adult poor may be lodged to whom this mode of maintenance is suited. They include, not only a large number of the infirm and incapable, but particularly all the good-for-nothings and depraved people who become a burden on public charity, whose conduct is a cause of annoyance, and who cannot be improved except by systematic discipline, by work, wholesome food and regular life." In fact, one great object was to clear the streets of Berne of the lazy and immoral of both sexes—people who could not, in a democratic country, be arbitrarily packed off to a prison, yet who were rightly regarded as social pests. The first of these two classes certainly far outweighs the second, but the second is by no means a small one. To this extent the Poorhouse has much in common with the Cantonal Labour Houses already referred to.

The number of persons who entered or passed through the Poorhouse during the year 1908 was as follows:—

	Males.	Females.	Total
Detained on January 1	202	152	354
Admitted during the year	54	24	78
Discharged during the year	36	26	62
Detained on December 31	220	150	370

Of those admitted during the year, seven were sent because of feeble-mindedness, twenty-two because of bad behaviour, seven because of unemployment, twenty-nine because of age and sickness, and thirteen were convalescents needing care in the country.

By reason of the large number of persons who flock to the town of Berne from various parts of the Canton and thus unduly swell the inmates of the Poorhouse, the Cantonal Government makes a liberal annual contribution to the costs of maintenance. Communes other than Berne which send persons to the Poorhouse for care or discipline pay from £10 to £12 per head.

The Poorhouse is situated several miles out of Berne, in a sequestered spot at the head of a fertile valley, affording just the isolation and means of effective oversight which are desirable in such a case. Attached to it are some 150 acres of land, which are divided into corn land, meadow and pasture land, plantation, and a large piece of land set apart as kitchen and nursery gardens. The building, which was intended to accommodate about 400 inmates—some fifty more than the usual complement—is a plain but substantial erection, and the arrangement of the various departments has been admirably thought out. In no way is there association between men and women, who both live and work in separate suites of rooms.

Work is required of all inmates according to their capacity. The regulations state:—

> "Every inmate is required to perform, to the extent of his power and ability, all such work as the director may assign or cause to be assigned to him, whether field work or employment in the workshops. The ordinary work day consists of ten hours, but in times of heavy field work (like harvest), the hours are according to needs. Sundays and general festivals are observed as days of rest, except that the inmates are required to do the necessary work in the house and farm buildings; only in urgent cases (like harvest), is other work required to be done on these days."

Whenever possible a man is set to the trade or occupation which he has been accustomed to follow. For farm labourers and gardeners, for example, there is always a place. Where inmates have had no particular training, the occupation in which they are likeliest to be most productive is allotted to them. Thus I noticed at work: smiths, wheelwrights, cabinet-makers, straw-plaiters, tailors, shoe makers, sempstresses, chair makers, wicker workers, bakers, paper bag makers, etc. Almost everything needed in the Colony in the nature of food, furniture, wood-work in general, tools, sewing, and knitting, besides repairs of all kinds, is produced on the spot, and at the time of my visit looms were on order for plain cloth weaving. In addition, a considerable sum is realised annually by the sale of articles made by the inmates and by the farming of their labour. The goods sold include chairs, wicker-work of various kinds, articles of straw, and paper bags. The farm is, however, still more productive. Of the daily production of between 300 and 350 quarts of milk, over one-half is consumed or used for butter, while the rest goes to the Co-operative Dairy of a neighbouring village, there to be turned into marketable cheese.

The dietary is largely vegetarian. Breakfast consists of coffee (always with milk), bread, and potatoes (or porridge once or twice a week instead of potatoes); dinner of soup and vegetables, with potatoes or farinaceous pudding and bread, meat being given twice or thrice a week; and supper of soup and bread, or coffee with bread or potatoes, a piece of cheese or other extra being added on Sunday evening. Inmates at work receive, in addition, both in the forenoon and the afternoon, bread with coffee, but cider or wine may be given instead of coffee in summer. On festivals a glass of wine is given at dinner.

No special uniform is used in the Poor-house. The inmates are attired in ordinary dress, without any attempt at symmetry, though deserters, when returned, are stamped on the coat as a warning.

The mental and recreative faculties of the inmates are not neglected, for thanks to the kindness of private persons, books, magazines, and newspapers are provided in considerable number.

It may be asked how order is maintained in a Colony so heterogeneous as this. The answer is that though the Municipal Authorities possess powers of punishment irrespective of the police, these powers have seldom to be exercised. A strong administrator, humane, but firm, who expects honest work from his people and therefore gets it, keeps the wheels of this notable piece of disciplinary machinery in smooth and regular rotation from year's end to year's end. Such of the inmates as can be trusted are even allowed to spend half a day in town once a week without any supervision whatever, and the privilege is seldom abused. They know, in fact, that they are under restraint until they have given proof of reformed habits, and that in the event of misconduct they will draw upon themselves more stringent restrictions. I believe that their amenability to discipline and obedience is but another proof that the besetting sin of the loafer is less active criminal propensity—save in so far as "oft the sight of means to do ill deeds makes ill deeds done"—than a corrigible laziness and disorderliness of life. To quote the words of the Director of the institution, as spoken to myself: "The people come here, as a rule, miserable and unhealthy, low and wretched, worn out by careless living and bad food, but they soon become new creatures." They do not all turn out saints by any means, but the percentage of wastrels won back to sobriety and industry is held far to outweigh the moderate maintenance expenditure incurred on their behalf.

The merely disciplinary measures which, in case of need, are taken against refractory inmates, include the assignment to them of hard and unpleasant work either in the house, the farmyard, the forest, or the fields, refusal of permission to leave the precincts of the establishment, and refusal of permission to receive visitors. The actual punishments which may be administered increase from reprimand in the case of misdemeanour to simple detention for a term not exceeding ten days, with or without bread and water every second day in the case of gross misdemeanour, and in aggravated cases detention in a separate room with marked clothing and close supervision. Corporal punishment is forbidden; the straight-jacket may be used only for the restraint of violent offenders, but not as a punishment, and it may only be applied for four hours at a time. Further, the Poor Law Authority has the right to transfer dangerous persons to another establishment.

On the other hand, the rewards for good conduct include the assignment to an inmate of a superior sleeping place, improved food rations, the payment of premiums, permission to leave the institution on Sunday, and appointment to posts of confidence.

The Poor-house is carried on very economically. The entire expenditure in 1908 amounted to £5,254, of which £454 represented the costs of administration, £3,721 the costs of maintenance, and £1,081 interest on capital. The revenue from agriculture was £1,452, from industry £500, and the maintenance charges and Cantonal subsidy amounted to £2,998, leaving a deficit of £306 to be made up by the municipality. Towards a total cost of £15 per head per annum, the inmates earned by agricultural and industrial work £5 11s. per head, leaving the net cost, all expenditure counted, £9 9s. per head per annum, or 3s. 8d. per week.

CHAPTER X.

LABOUR DEPOTS AND HOSTELS.

Although legislation in Germany and Switzerland is severe upon the vagrant loafers, generous provision is made in those countries for *bona fide* seekers of work. This is done by the complementary systems of public and semi-public Relief Stations and Hostels or popular lodging-houses. The Relief Stations are plain places of entertainment at which passing workmen, if duly accredited, may obtain food and a night's lodging in return for a certain task of work. In Germany they are established and maintained by the Provincial, District, or Communal Authorities, or by all three in conjunction, and where properly organised, as in Westphalia and South Germany, they are located at intervals which do not overtax the walking powers of men of ordinary capacity. The methods upon which the Stations are conducted are best explained by the rules of the Westphalian Federation of Relief Stations, which are as follows:—

> "(1) Every wayfarer not possessing more than one mark (1s.) in money, and unable to obtain work in the locality, will be considered as 'without means.' Any person who has more than one shilling in his possession, and who conceals or denies this fact, may not only be required to pay for the relief which he receives, but may also be prosecuted for fraud.

> "(2) Any person, who, by reason of old age, sickness, or infirmity, is unfit for work, will be referred to the local authorities with a view to his receiving Poor Law relief.

> "(3) Every wayfarer without means who wishes to receive relief in a relief station is required to produce his travelling pass. The wayfarer is required, provided that he is still in possession of any money, to procure such a pass himself. A pass may be obtained by the payment of 6d., or by the performance of at least four hours' work in the relief station. Relief is not given at the station issuing the pass. [This provision applies only to wayfarers able to pay.] A pass may only be issued to persons at least sixteen years of age, who are in a position, by producing a removal certificate or other similar evidence, to establish their identity, and are able to prove by means of insurance receipt, certificate of employment, etc., that they have recently been in work.

"Wayfarers who apply for relief at a relief station, but are not in possession of a travelling pass, will first be referred to the police as being 'homeless persons.' Only when the local police authorities certify that they have performed, with due industry, a task of work set by such authorities, and of at least one day's duration, and that no other objection exists to the issue of a travelling pass, can such pass be issued, and such persons be admitted to the regular relief offered by the station. [Persons relieved as 'homeless' are received into the relief station on the first or second day, according as the police require them to work for one day or two days, after completion of their work, and on the following morning they work for such a period as is prescribed by the rules of the station in return for the relief received by them, and then receive their pass.]

"The pass and all the other documents must be given up to the proper authorities of the relief station, and will be returned only after the required task of work has been performed.

"When a pass is issued, a note to that effect will be stamped on the other documents belonging to the holder. The stamp will show the place and date of the issue of the pass. An insurance receipt may not be stamped.

"(4) At each relief station, the wayfarer's pass shall be stamped with the date of his departure, which shall be evidence that the holder has completed the last section of his journey according to regulations, that he has not refused any work offered to him, and has performed the task assigned to him at the station according to regulations.

"The hour of departure and the name of the next station to which the holder proposes to travel must on every occasion be entered on his pass.

"(5) The holder of a pass is not allowed to make, or permit to be made, any entry in the same. Any such falsification, as also the use of the pass by any person other than the one to whom it was issued, is punishable (Penal Code, Section 363.)

"(6) The managers of travellers' hostels and of relief stations are authorised to confiscate any pass of which an improper use shall have been made.

"The cardinal principle to be observed is 'Work in the morning, travel in the afternoon.' Relief at a relief station will only be given if the man's pass contains the stamp of the station of departure dated on the same day as his application, and only at the station of destination. The traveller must arrive within such a time after his departure as is consistent with the distance from the station of departure, and with the hour of his departure entered upon the pass.

"(7) In special cases, especially in winter, and if the nearest station where the night is to be spent is more than five hours' walk from the station of departure, a wayfarer may be allowed to leave in the forenoon, and be given a meal before his departure. Whenever long distances have to be traversed, light refreshment or an order for a meal at some intermediate place (substation) may also be supplied.

"(8) Employment maybe sought only through the intervention of the Labour Registry in connection with the relief station. Going about in search of work is prohibited.

"Anyone refusing to accept a suitable situation when offered will not be eligible for work and relief at a relief station.

"If a situation cannot be found for a man, he is required to perform the work allotted to him at the relief station. The nature and the duration of this work are determined by the manager of the station. By accepting relief, the wayfarer undertakes the obligation to perform the work allotted to him, and to comply with the regulations in force at the station. Any man, accepting relief, who afterwards refuses to work and leaves the station without permission will be prosecuted for fraud.

"(9) Wayfarers who, by reason of their having failed to comply with these regulations, have to be refused relief, and who are destitute, will be referred to the local authorities. Any man who arrives too late shall not be admitted at the relief station, but shall be referred to the police authorities for further relief. On the following morning, he will be required, in exchange for the relief provided for him by the police, to perform a task of work; and at noon he must have his pass stamped at the relief station with the words 'Relieved by the Police,' and thereupon he will again become subject to the regulations for travelling workmen. Any man whose pass does not show the proper continuous sequence of stamps, and who is unable to give a satisfactory explanation of the fact, will be treated as if he did not possess a pass. Any man who may be found in localities or on roads other than those mentioned on the map displayed at the relief station, is liable to be punished as a vagrant wandering without reasonable cause.

"(10) On Sundays and other days recognised by the Federation of Relief Stations as holidays, rest and relief (including a mid-day meal) will be allowed in the forenoon to all such persons as arrived the day before at the right time, and with their passes in order. It is expected that every man will attend the religious service of the confession to which he belongs. In the afternoon the men will proceed on their journeys."

Hitherto the Provincial Diet of Westphalia has borne one-third of the cost of the Relief Stations in the Province, and the remainder has fallen on the District and Communal Authorities. During the year October 1, 1907 to September 30, 1908, 116,995 persons were helped on the way by these institutions, and the total cost was £5,655.

A system of Relief Stations of this kind must cover a given area completely in order to realise its purpose, which is to assist destitute wayfarers to travel in search of work without being under the necessity of begging. The best developed system yet in existence is weakened by gaps here and there, and it was with a view to perfecting the network of Stations in Prussia that the Government of that country, on the initiative of Pastor von Bodelschwingh, passed the law of June 29, 1907, for the establishment of Labour Depots for travelling work-people (*Wanderarbeitsstättengesetz*). This novel law gives power to the Diets of Provinces to require urban and rural districts (circles) to establish, maintain, and administer Labour Depots; such decisions must be supported by a majority of two-thirds of the votes given. It is the purpose of these Labour Depots to "procure work for destitute able-bodied men who are in search of employment away from their place of residence, and meantime to provide them with food and lodging in return for a task of labour." Districts in which Depots are not established may be required to contribute to the cost of Depots elsewhere by which they benefit. While the cost of the Depots falls, in the first instance, on the Districts, the Provinces must refund to them two-thirds of the costs, and the State contributes to the cost of all Labour Registries carried on in connection with Depots.

Communes in which Depots are established must co-operate with the Districts in their management, and on payment must provide suitable buildings, so far as these have hitherto been used for the same purpose.

A fully organised Labour Depot, as contemplated by this law, comprises, in addition to a workshop or workyard, a Hostel in which work-seekers are lodged and fed in return for a task of work, and a Labour Registry. It is not necessary that either Hostel or Registry should be carried on independently of existing institutions of the kind so long as these are efficient and it is possible to come to a satisfactory working arrangement with them.

It is required that the work to be performed shall entail real exertion, yet be suited to every man's capacity, and as far as possible be in keeping with his normal occupation. As to the food supplied, it is stipulated that it shall be simple yet "so abundant that the wayfarer may remain capable of walking and working and may not be compelled to beg on the way." The admission of wayfarers to Labour Depots and their travelling from one Depot to another are to be regulated by rules issued by the Provincial Authorities.

Already the law has been put in operation in Westphalia and several other parts of Prussia. The regulations adopted by the Provincial Authorities of Westphalia follow closely those which have hitherto governed the system of Relief Stations there. The Depots only admit males of at least sixteen years, who are destitute and capable of work, and are in search of work away from their place of residence, but a legal right to admission is not recognised. Any wayfarer who does not possess more than one mark (1s.) in money, and cannot find work in his locality is deemed to be destitute in the sense of the law; a man in receipt of adequate travelling benefit is not regarded as destitute, and anyone who has more than a mark and conceals the fact is required to pay for his keep, and is liable to prosecution for fraud. The pass or way-ticket used is substantially the same as that of the German Hostel Association (*Herbergsverein*), and the conditions of its issue are: (1) Possession of a certificate of removal from the Police Authorities of the last place of residence, and an insurance receipt card; (2) possession of official labour certificates, such as a sickness insurance card, showing that the bearer has worked at least six weeks during the preceding three months, or has been incapable of work during that time; (3) the payment of 50 pfennige (6d.) or the performance of one and a half days of work in the Depot for the way-ticket. Men who have been discharged from the army, from Labour Houses, or from prison need only produce their discharge papers, instead of documents 1 and 2 during the first four weeks after such discharge. A way-ticket and other documents of identification must be produced, and the former must be stamped, at each Depot visited.

The labour task imposed lasts a day and a half or twelve hours, and the wayfarer may go on his journey after dinner on the third day, provided his task be completed, but when the pressure of inmates is great he may be discharged half a day sooner, *i.e.*, on the morning of the third day, and the same relief may be given when the distance to the next Depot exceeds five hours of walking. Food may be given to be eaten on the way, or a ticket for the same may be given instead. Where the distance is very far, where a Labour Colony or a hospital is the objective, and in case of bad weather or physical unfitness, the wayfarer may be given a free railway ticket. Admission is refused, and the way-ticket may be forfeited, if a wayfarer presents himself a second time within six months at the same Depot. Should a way-ticket be withdrawn, a pass to a Voluntary Labour Colony may be issued instead, and after four weeks' work there, or in a similar institution recognised by the Provincial Authority, a new ticket may be issued. Wayfarers who are not, for any reason, admitted to a Depot must be referred to the local authorities as homeless. Such a man, on producing a certificate from these authorities to the effect that he has performed the work assigned to him for two days, and has applied to the police of his last place of residence for a removal certificate and an insurance receipt card, may be maintained in the local Depot until noon of the sixth work-day in return for eight hours of work a day; should the removal certificate arrive in the interval a way-ticket may be issued to him, and in the event of its non-arrival, the Depot may apply to the police to issue a new insurance receipt card. If the removal certificate is not produced, the wayfarer receives a pass to a Voluntary Labour Colony at noon on the sixth work day.

It is proposed to introduce a system of Labour Depots in Wurtemberg on the Prussian model, and an Association has been formed to this end. The work to be offered will be street and road making and cleaning, garden and field work, stone breaking, wood cutting, etc. Lodgings will be found for the wayfarer in neighbouring Hostels where they exist, or else in Poorhouses, hospitals, or private houses.

Bavaria is already provided with a large and efficient network of public Labour Depots and Relief Stations for the benefit of wayfarers. Their number in 1904 was 347, of which 150 were maintained by the District Authorities, 113 by the Communal Authorities, and 84 by associations. In that year the Depots relieved 644,556 persons, of whom 328,201 lodged for the night, 32,978 were agricultural labourers, 353,356 were artisans, 46,950 builders' or other labourers, 41,007 factory operatives, 14,074 commercial assistants, and 156,191 followed miscellaneous or unknown occupations. The year's aggregate expenditure was £16,652 and the income £17,533, of which £3,795 was received from private persons, £12,066 from District and

Communal Authorities, £169 from trade guilds and similar associations, and £305 from miscellaneous societies.

The working men's Hostels, on the other hand, while fulfilling the same purpose as the Relief Stations, are carried on by philanthropic societies, generally with public help from various sources. They are decent lodging-houses which, as a rule, admit several classes of persons—wayfarers who are able to pay for the accommodation afforded, those who perform a task of work instead of paying money, and boarders of a more or less permanent kind. Travellers who receive board and lodging in return for work are required to identify themselves by means of a formal way-ticket, which can be obtained at the cost of a day's labour. I have visited many of these Hostels in all parts of Germany, and it is impossible to speak too highly of them. They are quiet and decorous houses of call, where wandering toilers rest and are thankful for the kindly care, the thoughtful foresight, and the paternal solicitude which minister to their well-being. With these "homes from home" to resort to, the respectable workman may make the entire circuit of the country, if needful, under conditions that do not weaken his morality and self-respect. Above all, they give him the opportunity of keeping out of the current of promiscuous humanity—composed of elements so largely degraded, baneful, and turbulent—which is expressed by the pregnant word "trampdom."

I cannot do better than enumerate the conditions upon which the way-ticket of the German Hostel Association (an organisation with ramifications in every part of the Empire), is issued since it is accepted by the Police Authorities everywhere as an official document, the exhibition of which protects the possessor against the undesirable attentions of perambulating constables on the look-out for idle mendicants. It is a principle of the association to regard as "without means," and therefore proper subjects for help, any workman who has no more than 1s. in his pocket, and is unable to find employment in the town where he happens to be located. Such a man is received to the full benefits of the Association without formality or fee, though if by reason of age, sickness, or physical infirmity of any kind, he should be unfit for the road, or for work, the services of the Poor Law Authorities are enlisted on his behalf. Thus, a workless artisan or labourer, desirous of going in search of employment, can at once obtain a way-ticket on proof given of his *bona fides*, and so equipped he is able to walk any necessary distance without cost to himself. An official of the local Hostel—for most towns of importance possess at least one—helps him to draw up his plan of route, which is so arranged that after five or six hours of moderate walking each day, he may land at the door of a hospitable Shelter, where food, lodging, and due care for his moral welfare await him. No superfluous *detours* are allowed; the route chosen is as direct as possible, and is only conditioned by the existence on the way of the necessary places of call. Though the entertainment offered is without money, however, it is not without price; the price being several hours of light employment, suited to the man's character and capacity, before the day's march begins; nevertheless, the task may be omitted where circumstances justify it. The wayfarer may present himself at the Hostel as soon in the afternoon as he likes, but he must not turn up later than seven o'clock. On Sunday no work is required, but a religious service takes its place, though in the afternoon the men are sent on their way as on any other day.

Many of these lodging-houses serve simultaneously as Labour Registries, or are associated with such agencies, in which case an attempt is made to provide work for such wandering workmen as are not particular as to their destination. Should suitable employment be offered, it must be accepted on pain of forfeiting claim to further help from the Association and its shelters. Without a way-ticket no one is admitted to a Hostel. This document is handed in immediately on arrival, and is retained until the owner's departure the following day. In the meantime, it is stamped in a place provided for the purpose with the date and the name of the station, and the name of the succeeding station is added in writing by way of direction to the wanderer. The personal data which are entered on the way-ticket are certainly sufficient in number and detail to prevent abuse and fraud. Besides name, place, and date of birth, occupation, last place of work, and religious confession, they include the man's height, the colour of his eyes and hair and the shape of his face, and other notable traits can be added at the Directors discretion.

In 1908 the number of Hostels affiliated to the German Hostel Association was 454. During the year 2,622,000 persons were received in the Hostels for 4,547,028 nights, an increase of 551,922 persons and 483,818 nights as compared with 1907. Of those housed, 1,871,271 paid for their accommodation, 716,273 worked in return for it (these 2,587,544 persons being workpeople in transit), and 34,456 were more or less permanent boarders. Work was found by the Hostel Labour Registries for 139,088 persons.

Great as is the value of these two types of institutions in helping the unemployed to obtain work, they perform a further useful service in removing from such people the temptation to mendicancy, and in clearing off the mere loafers. For it is a significant fact that the establishment of public Relief Stations has invariably had the same effect upon the tramp which the hardening of casual ward discipline has had in England; where Relief Stations have appeared the tramp has disappeared, for the simple reason that their existence gave him no excuse for begging, while the work which they offered him was not to his mind. Herr von Massow, a prominent worker in the German Relief Station movement, writes:—

> "When the system was carefully adopted in wide areas the success was great and auspicious. The itinerant population of the highways greatly decreased, and the houses of correction were empty. It must not be assumed, however, that the vagrants quite abandoned the highways; they rather migrated to districts in which there were no relief stations, and large numbers crossed over the frontier, into Holland, Austria, France, and even Italy."[67]

According to Pastor von Bodelschwingh, vagabondage has almost disappeared in those districts of Westphalia in which a rational system of Relief Stations and Hostels has been established. He quotes the Local Authority of Herford as saying that "since the regulation of the way-ticket and Hostel system, the vagrancy and begging nuisance has almost ceased; our boundary inspectors have officially confirmed this." The same effect has followed from the same cause in South Germany. The monthly journal of the German Hostel Association recently stated that:—

> "The development of the relief stations created eighteen or twenty years ago has led to the establishment of a central station at Constance, which has been attended by great success. Street and house begging has almost disappeared, and the cases of robbery and theft have greatly diminished."[68]

In Switzerland provision is made for wayfarers on much the same lines. Work-seekers possessed of the recognised papers of identification are, on application, supplied by the police with food and lodging, or they may apply to the depots maintained with Government help by the Inter-cantonal Union of Relief Stations. This Union now covers fourteen out of the twenty-two Cantons of the Confederation and its Relief Stations are modelled after the German pattern. In many places accommodation is provided for the wayfarer at the police stations, at others inns and private houses are used; the number of special Hostels is small. Contrary to the practice of the German Relief Stations, however, work is not necessarily required in return for the food and lodging given; if the applicants are regarded as genuine work-seekers they are sent on their way as soon as possible. The official Relief Stations work hand in hand with employment registries and other agencies in the towns, in the endeavour to procure suitable work for those who desire it locally. New garments and shoes are often given to those who need them.

The regulations of the Relief Stations do not differ greatly from those in force in Westphalia, as already quoted in full. A wayfarer desiring relief is required first to have his papers "controlled" or examined, and this is done in many cases at the police station. The examination satisfactory, he receives a stamped and dated ticket entitling him to admission to a Station; his name, calling, age and ordinary place of residence being entered in a register for record and future reference. As a rule, no relief is given if the applicant proves not to have been in work within the preceding three months, and if he refuses the work offered to him, though exceptions are frequently made. A wayfarer is only given food or lodging once in six months at the same Station. When he goes on his way he takes with him a stamped and dated way-ticket, which he must present at the next place at which he stops, but he must travel at least two hours from one Station to another in order to qualify again for relief. In case of any abuse of relief, infringement of the regulations concerning lodging, or failure to produce valid papers, the applicant is handed over to the police. Every person carrying a wayfarer's book must have a certificate from his employer stating the date of last employment, and the signature of the employer must be authenticated by the local police or by the stamp of the Relief Station.

Summarising the operations of all the Relief Stations affiliated to the Inter-cantonal Union, I find that during 1908, 180,246 persons were relieved, 128,859 being lodged for the night, and 51,387 receiving dinner only. The cost of the Stations was £7,100, of which maintenance represented £5,380. The State contributions towards the expenditure amounted to £2,820, or 40 per cent. of the whole. It appears that 5,625 applicants for relief were referred to the police, and that the waytickets of 117 were confiscated. Of the persons relieved 14·1 per cent. were under twenty years of age, 35·8 per cent. were between twenty and thirty years, 19·8 per cent. were between thirty and forty years, 15·6 per cent. were between forty and fifty, 10·5 per cent. between fifty and sixty, and 4·1 per cent. were above sixty years. Employment was found for 5,356 of the wayfarers by means of the Labour Registries attached to the Stations.

As in Germany, so in Switzerland, it has been found that the existence of these Relief Stations, far from encouraging vagabondage, has exactly the opposite effect, thanks to the stringent control which is exercised. The genuine seeker after work knows that he can claim accommodation free, while the idle vagabond knows that his non-possession of a way-ticket inferentially proclaims him to be a pest, whose proper place is the Labour House, and he makes himself scarce. Excellent as is the work done by the Relief Stations, however, it is held that they will be still more efficient when private enterprise, where it still exists, is superseded by public organisation and administration, and this is the inevitable goal of the system. It is obvious that only when the Stations altogether pass into the care of the Administrative Authorities will it be possible to secure that uniformity of management which is so desirable. It is also probable that more will be done to bring the Stations into closer relationship with the labour organisations. Each may be regarded as complementary, the one to the other, though it has not hitherto been possible to secure systematic co-operation between them.

CHAPTER XI.

RECOMMENDATIONS OF RECENT COMMISSIONS.

It is now desirable to review the attitude towards this question of three Commissions who have considered and reported upon it during the past seven years—the Viceregal Poor Law Reform Commission for Ireland, appointed in 1903, the Departmental Committee on Vagrancy appointed by the President of the Local Government Board in July, 1904, and the Royal Commission on the Poor Law, appointed in December, 1905.

The Irish Viceregal Commission, in their Report published in 1906, came to the following conclusions:—

> "Our opinion agrees with that of the majority of witnesses examined before us, that people who are travelling about the country without employment, without any means of their own, and who have to support themselves by mendicancy or recourse to the Poor Law, or by sleeping out, should be brought by the police before a court of justice. If they could not then, or through the police or other agency after remand, give satisfactory evidence (documentary or other), to the court, of their being habitually hard working and self-supporting, there should, we suggest, be power conferred upon a Court of Jurisdiction to direct them to a Labour House in which the inmates should, as is said to be the case in Belgian establishments, be required to make or produce the food, clothing and necessaries for such an institution. We think that, at all events to begin with, four such Labour Houses might be established for Ireland, and that four disused workhouses might be set apart for the purpose."[69]

It may be observed here that the Royal Commissioners who inquired into the working of the Irish Poor Law in 1833 recommended, in their Report of 1836, that the able-bodied paupers should be employed in the reclamation of waste land, in works of drainage and fencing, and in the building of improved dwellings. They also recommended the establishment of penitentiaries for vagrants, and the deportation of suitable persons as free labourers to a non-penal Colony. Substantially this was the method of treating loafers practised in Holland at that time.

The Vice-Regal Commission enumerated the following classes of people as suited to detention in Labour Houses:—

(1) Rural vagrants over fifteen years of age.

(2) Urban loafers over fifteen years of age.

(3) Mothers of two or more illegitimate children except when nursing infants.

(4) All parents who are unfit to be entrusted with the charge of their children, except mothers nursing infants.

(5) Any able-bodied soldiers or ex-solders who are not self-supporting or are not supported by the Military Authorities.

(6) Any able-bodied adult persons who may, at the instance of the police or the local Poor Law Authority, be considered by a Court of Justice as proper cases, owing to their failure to support themselves.

(7) Destitute able-bodied adults who may voluntarily desire to be admitted as inmates; and

(8) Any destitute able-bodied adults who may be offered an order of admission to a Labour House by Poor Law Authorities or their officials in the prescribed manner, *i.e.*, as a test of destitution.[70]

As to the character of the Labour Houses proposed, the Report of the Commission states:—

> "We should be sorry to see in them anything suggestive of more comfort than can be derived from very hard work, enough of simple food, clean healthy buildings, fittings and surroundings, but everything of the plainest, roughest kind. After the first starting and equipment of the Labour House we think that the inmates, all of whom would be able-bodied, ought to be obliged to rely, as far as possible, on their own labours for their support, and as a stimulus they should be individually made to feel the necessity for personal exertion."[71]

The Commission further proposed that these Houses of Detention should be provided and administered by the General Prisons Board and their cost be defrayed by the National Treasury.

The English Committee on Vagrancy was the immediate outcome of the more active interest taken in Poor Law circles in the question of vagrant regulation during the years 1901 to 1904, and of the great increase in vagrancy which took place during the trade depression of three of those years.

It must be remembered that the Vagrancy Committee were called upon to inquire into the case of wayfarers exclusively; nevertheless, some of their recommendations are equally applicable to loafers of other classes.

The terms of reference were—"To inquire and report with respect to England and Wales as to (1) the law applicable to persons of the vagrant class (*i.e.*, the statutory provisions and the bye-laws, rules, and regulations made thereunder); (2) the administration of the law applicable to these persons; and (3) any amendments which should be made in it or in its administration."

The findings of the Committee are crystallised in the words: "It is clear to us that the present system neither repels nor reforms the vagrant."

The negative and positive recommendations which were embodied in the Committee's Report, a document marked by exceptional ability and breadth of view, may be briefly summarised as follows. This Report is the more important since the Poor Law Commission, wisely abstaining from further inquiries into this aspect of Poor Law administration, substantially endorsed the conclusions of the Vagrancy Committee and the remedial measures based upon them.

The Committee accept the view that the relief of vagrants should be altogether removed from the jurisdiction of the Poor Law and be entrusted to the police, adding:—

> "We have considered in detail the difficulties in the way of this change, and on the whole, we see no reason to doubt that if the importance of effecting it is once realised, the necessary adjustments can be made without serious friction."[72]

In sympathy with this view the Committee would empower the police to provide lodging for genuine wayfarers, but they would detain habitual vagrants in Forced Labour Colonies.

> "Our view is that means should be provided to allow of the habitual vagrant being dealt with otherwise than under the Vagrancy Act, and that as far as possible, he should be treated not as a criminal, but as a person requiring detention on account of his mode of life. This is the principle which governs the system adopted in Belgium under the law of 1891. For this purpose we propose that a class of habitual vagrants should be defined by statute, and that this class should include any person who has been three or more times convicted during a period of, say, twelve months of certain offences now coming under the Vagrancy Act, namely, sleeping out, begging, refusing to perform task of work in casual wards, or refusing or neglecting to maintain himself so that he becomes chargeable to the poor rate. It will be seen that we do not propose to create any new

> offence, and that under the existing law, this class could be dealt with as incorrigible rogues. Under this proposal, a means is provided of enabling the Poor Law authorities to deal with the class of "ins and outs" who now cause considerable trouble in workhouse administration. We suggest that persons coming within this definition should be committed by a petty sessional court to quarter sessions or assizes, and there dealt with in the same way as the incorrigible rogue, with the exception that the sentence should be committed to a labour colony for a term not exceeding three years."[73]

The Committee further endorse the objections to short sentences which have been advanced times without number by critics of the Vagrancy Laws, and propose that delinquents committed to the proposed Labour Colonies should be detained for not less than six months or more than three years, but that there should be power to curtail a sentence when a prisoner showed good conduct or earned a certain sum of money in wages, as is done at Merxplas.

> "The evidence we have received shows conclusively that from any practical point of view, it is impossible to defend a sentence of a few days. That it is in no way deterrent to the vagrant is the opinion of all the witnesses.... We are so fully convinced of the futility and needless expense of the short sentence, that we consider it necessary to urge that in any case, where the magistrate deems it expedient to give a sentence of less than fourteen days for a vagrancy offence, the sentence should be for one day only.... A sentence for one day means that the prisoner is detained until the rising of the court, and then discharged. Under our proposal this sentence would be a conviction; the conviction would be recorded, and the offender would be warned by the court that on his second or third conviction he would be imprisoned for a considerable period or, if our later recommendations are accepted, he would be committed for a still longer period of detention in a labour colony as a habitual vagrant."[74]

The Committee adopted my view that Voluntary Labour Colonies of the German type are useless for persons of the loafing class.

> "It is clear that a labour colony of the German type is of little use for dealing with persons of the tramp class. Mr. Dawson says that 'it is not disciplinary in the coercive sense:

> it is purely voluntary; the inmates can stay or not as they please.' Many of this type of colonists come again and again, and are termed 'colony loafers.' They correspond to the 'ins-and-outs' of our English workhouses. The object of the colonies is to effect some moral reformation, but it appears that three-fourths of the colonists have been previously imprisoned, and there is no evidence that any substantial improvement results from the time spent in the colonies. Mr. Dawson expresses his opinion thus:—
>
> 'Speaking generally, I do not think that you can regard them as being reformatory institutions. The inmates do not stay long enough and the discipline is not severe enough.'"[75]

They also include the existing English Labour Colonies in the same criticism. "None of these Colonies," they say, "is intended primarily for persons actually belonging to the vagrant class; there is no power of detention, and the conditions are generally superior to what would be desirable in a Colony to which habitual vagrants would be committed."[76]

The Committee further agree that a purely agricultural Colony is altogether inferior to one in which trades and industries are carried on in conjunction with farm work, and that only on this twofold basis can a Labour Colony be conducted economically and efficiently.

> "Apart from the fact that agriculture alone would not pay, the experience of labour colonies is that agriculture could not be relied upon as the sole employment for the colonists: on wet days throughout the year, in frosty weather, and, indeed, during a great part of the winter, but little farm work could be carried on; again, some of the colonists would be quite unfitted for work of this character; and, lastly, there would be difficulty in disposing of the surplus agricultural produce without affecting outside industries. Everywhere the managers of colonies have found it necessary to establish workshops and various kinds of indoor industries in addition to work on the land, and it seems clear that the organisation of indoor industries must take the foremost place in a colony if employment has to be found for a large body of colonists all the year round."[77]

Very wisely and necessarily, too, the Committee have called attention to a danger which, unless closely watched, would discredit past redemption any public Detention Colonies that might be established in this country—the danger of launching into extravagant, foolish, and needless expenditure on buildings and initial installation.

> "We are strongly of opinion that as regards any buildings coming within our proposals, means should be adopted to protect the ratepayer from any expenditure that is not really necessary for the object in view."[78]

The Committee would deal kindly with the private interests which may be expected to raise an outcry against Labour Colony competition in the labour market. While, however, they would restrict competition with free industry as far as possible, they add the reservation that on that principle free labour would not have to compete with the Colonies—in other words, the latter should have a right to supply, if able, the whole of their own needs.

The Committee would adopt in full the Continental practice of allowing the inmates to earn wages out of which to supplement their food rations and to save for the day of release.

> "We realise the futility of establishing labour colonies for the reformation of the habitual vagrant unless some means can be devised of making him work: and it would be undesirable to have to resort to constant punishment to enforce the performance of the daily task. The punishments, too, would be limited; bread and water diet could not be given continually, and confinement to a cell would probably soon lose its effect. Compulsion, therefore, would in some cases be impossible, and the inducements to good conduct and industry which are held out to the inmates of prisons, such as letters or visits from their friends, classification indicating superiority of some kind, and so on, would scarcely appeal to the majority of the inmates of a vagrant colony. We believe that the best and simplest method of securing the desired end would be to allow the colonists to earn by industry and good conduct small sums of money, a portion of which should be retained until their discharge, and a portion handed over to them weekly to spend, if they like, at the canteen of the colony in the purchase of extra articles of food, tobacco, etc.; and the accumulation of a certain amount of earnings might afford an opportunity for earlier discharge."[79]

It is worthy of note that the Merxplas theory of social reinstatement is virtually embraced by the Committee, who say:—

> "In the case of labour colonies, much expense in the way of buildings and staff can be saved by adopting the view

accepted at Merxplas, that it is not worth while to go to great expense in preventing the escape of the inmates. If a colonist escapes, and is able to support himself without coming within the reach of the law, his escape from the colony is no matter for regret; if he breaks the law and comes again before a magistrate a proper system of identification will ensure his being sent back to the colony. If the detention is intended not so much as a punishment, but rather as a means of restraining the vagrant from his debased mode of life, the risk of his escaping need not be regarded so seriously as in the case of a criminal committed to prison to expiate his crime."

Considering the question of finding employment for discharged prisoners, the Committee recommend that the superintendent of each police division should be responsible for the collection of information as to work available in his district, and that this information should be transmitted at frequent intervals to the chief constable of the county, who would send complete lists to each police station and to the casual wards for the inspection of those seeking work. This recommendation was made before the decision to establish State labour registries in all the large towns. Where this new machinery exists it would clearly be expedient to use it, and for that purpose it would be necessary for each Labour Colony to keep in constant touch with the nearest official registry, receiving its periodical lists of vacant situations, and notifying such reliable labour as it may have at disposal. The public labour registries would in this way be helpful in assisting discharged inmates to find industrial employment, but in so far as agricultural work might be needed, the Colonies would probably have to rely upon their own sources of information.

When they come to discuss the authorities which should establish and be responsible for the maintenance of the Detention Colonies, some of the Committee's recommendations seem to me to call for reconsideration. They object to State-managed Colonies on the ground that the State would provide institutions of the wrong kind, and would be sure to establish either too many or too few,[80] and propose that the County Councils and voluntary philanthropic and religious agencies should be left both to establish and manage these institutions.

The County Councils alone are, in my opinion, the proper authorities to undertake this responsibility, and in entrusting it to them we should only be reverting to the practice of the sixteenth century, when the provision of places of work for vagrants was made incumbent upon Quarter Sessions in every county.

Moreover, I hold still to the view, advanced in my evidence before the Committee, that there is no warrant whatever for supposing that private enterprise and philanthropy would be willing to provide the funds necessary for establishing these Colonies. Nor, in my opinion, is there any reason why they should. The disciplinary treatment of the vagrant and the loafer is a public duty, and it cannot safely be left to private effort, however well-meaning that effort might be. The Voluntary Labour Colonies of the Continent and the English Colonies of the Salvation Army type rest rightly on a private basis, for their work is avowedly philanthropic and moral, and the men for whom they exist come and go at will. Detention Colonies, on the other hand, would be an essential part of the penal system of the country, and powers of restraint such as they would exercise could not properly be placed in the hands of private individuals or associations. I reassert the contention, therefore, that the Colonies should be provided by the counties according to requirements, the right being given to several counties to combine for the purpose, with a view to avoiding any unnecessary multiplication of establishments. At the same time private Colonies would prove useful auxiliaries to the public Colonies in the way indicated in the third chapter.[81]

One type of Colony alone the Committee would require the State to provide—a Colony strictly penal in character for the reception of bad cases.

> "Although we have recommended that labour colonies should be established and managed by county councils and voluntary agencies rather than by the State, we are of opinion that it may be necessary to have at least one institution under State control. It will no doubt be found that certain of the habitual vagrants will not be amenable to the discipline of the ordinary labour colonies, or from their repeated escapes, and re-committals will need a more severe treatment. We would suggest that instead of sending such cases to a prison, a labour colony of a penal type should be established by the State. This State labour colony should be conducted generally, on the lines of the ordinary labour colony, except that the discipline enforced should be more severe, and that escapes should be more carefully guarded against. It would also be necessary to secure that it did not possess attractions over the ordinary colonies, either in diet or other respects."[82]

They propose also that all Colonies, however established, should be certified by the Secretary of State, should be managed in accordance with regulations issued by him, and should be subject to inspection by officers appointed by him.

The Committee do not assent to the immediate abolition of the casual wards. "We see no likelihood," they write, "of its being possible to dispense altogether with casual wards for the reception of needy wayfarers, at all events for some years,"[83] though they propose to place them under the control of the police. As my own evidence is cited in favour of abolition, it may be advisable to say that as an alternative I suggested, as already explained,[84] the establishment of hostels superior to the casual wards for the accommodation of genuine work-seekers. I contend that the casual wards are too good for the vagabond and not nearly good enough for the honest worker. In Germany and Switzerland, as we have seen, accommodation equal to that of a decent working man's cottage can be had in public hostels by the certified wayfarer for the cost of a dirty bed in an English "model" lodging-house, and if the ratepayer were relieved of the heavy direct and indirect cost of maintaining the tramp, he would probably be willing to make provision on generous lines for respectable wayfarers desirous of finding employment.

Something may, indeed, be said in favour of abolishing the casual wards by degrees only, but the insuperable objection to their permanence is that to retain the wards would mean the retention and toleration of the tramp. It will be useless to wage war against vagrancy if we leave the enemy in quiet possession of his cover. In any event it is clear that until improved accommodation is provided for *bona fide* work-seekers, the casual wards will have to continue in some form. When such accommodation exists, however, and the tramp is given the alternative of work with freedom or work under restraint, the excuse for the casual ward will disappear.

Meantime, the Vagrancy Committee wish to see genuine seekers of work treated differently from the ordinary casuals, in having a merely nominal task of work to perform, instead of one of nine hours, in return for the relief given.

> "Some means," they say, "should be adopted of discriminating between the wayfarer who is genuinely in search of work and the idle vagrant. Nearly all the witnesses we have examined have expressed themselves in favour of some system of way-tickets as a means of helping the *bona fide* work-seeker on his way or of assisting to distinguish such a case from the undeserving mendicant. The proposal is one which has received general support. Although the *bona fide* work-seeker forms but a very small proportion of

> the total number of vagrants, it is impossible to exclude this class from any consideration of the vagrancy problem. The fact that under the present system the working man on tramp who goes to a casual ward receives just the same treatment there as the professional mendicant, is a direct encouragement to indiscriminate almsgiving, as persons who give to the beggar on the road have the excuse that he may be a *bona fide* work-seeker who ought not to be treated like the ordinary vagrant. We are strongly of opinion that some better provision should be made to assist the man genuinely in search of work, not only because his case merits different treatment, but because it is most important to remove the excuse for casual almsgiving. It appears that in the case of members of trades unions there is no need of any provision of this sort....
>
> "We propose the performance of a small task by the holder of a way-ticket. It may be urged that if the man is *bona fide* in search of work he should not be required to do any task; but we consider that a task of a useful but light nature will help to maintain a spirit of independence, and at the same time act as a check to any abuse of the facilities provided. In return for the food and lodging given, it seems only right that the recipient should do some work, but we think he should be free to do the work as soon as he wishes, either on the day of arrival or the next day, so that he can leave the ward as early as possible. For the way-ticket man we propose that there should practically be no detention, and we think that he should generally have better treatment and accommodation than the ordinary vagrants, and be kept as far as possible apart from them. And it should be open to him to remain at the ward for another night if he desires a rest on his journey."[85]

The passport or way-ticket system recommended by the Committee is substantially that which has been carried on for years in Westphalia[86] and other parts of Germany in connection with the Relief Stations, as already described, and upon which the Swiss system was modelled. The Committee say:—

> "We think that the police should be empowered to issue a way-ticket to a man who can satisfy them either that he has worked at some employment (other than a casual job)

within a recent period, say three months, and that he has reasonable ground for expecting to get work at a certain place, and that he is likely to keep to it, or that he has some other good ground for desiring to go to some particular place. A case that might be dealt with under the latter description is the sailor who has missed his ship, and wishes to get to some other port.

"The ticket should give the man's personal description, his usual trade, his reason for wanting to travel, and his proposed destination, and should contain his signature, and, possibly, his finger-prints for the purpose of testing his identity. It should be in the form of a book, something like the Swiss traveller's book, with spaces on which should be stamped the name of each casual ward visited. We think that the duration of the book should be limited to a certain period, say one month. With this book, the man would go to the casual ward, and be entitled to a night's lodging, supper, and breakfast, and, after performing two hours' work to help to pay for his food and lodging, he should be free to leave the ward whenever he likes. The name of the next ward on the direct line of his route, which he can reach that night, should be entered in the book, and if he arrived at that place he should be treated in the same manner. The book would thus be a record of the man's journey, and show clearly on the face of it whether he is genuinely in search for work."[87]

There would appear to be no reason, however, why the issue of way-tickets should be confined to the police, and the finger-print method of identification, which is well enough for rogues and vagabonds, would be an indignity in the case of *bona fide* working men. In both respects a certain degree of elasticity seems desirable. Way-tickets might be issued by the State labour registries, the Charity Organization Societies, and relieving officers, and in the case of organised workers by their trade unions, without reference to the police, and the less reputable class of way farers alone might be required to apply to the local police office.

The Poor Law Commission have virtually endorsed the Detention Colony proposals contained in the Report of the Vagrancy Committee, while giving them wider application. The Vagrancy Committee considered the vagrant alone; the Poor Law Commission considered him only in so far as he uses the casual wards and hence falls upon public charity, and even so quite incidentally as one among many types of mischievous paupers with whose case existing Poor Law methods and institutions are unable satisfactorily to deal. The recommendations of the Commission, therefore, cover a wide field, yet so far as measures of discipline and restraint go they coincide broadly with the proposals detailed in the earlier pages of this book.

The Commission say in the Majority Report:—

> "The last and most difficult class with which the Public Assistance Committee will have to deal are those who, before they have any chance of being restored to independence, require detention, discipline, and training for a prolonged period. We may subdivide this class into two divisions:—(1) Those unwilling to work; (2) those whose character and behaviour are such that no employer will engage them.... It does not seem to us that the maintenance and detention of persons who will not work, or whose recent character and conduct are an inseparable bar to their re-entering industrial life, are within the legitimate functions of a Public Assistance Authority. Detention under disciplinary treatment affords the best hope of their reformation, or of preventing them by their example or conduct from contaminating those with whom they come in contact. They should be handed over to that authority whose special duty it is to detain those whose presence at large is a mischief to the community. Detention Colonies under the control of the Home Office should, in our judgment, be established for the reception of this class. We believe that no system of labour or industrial colonies can be properly worked unless there is in reserve a semi-penal institution, to which those who refuse to comply with the rules and regulations of the colony can be sent upon proof of repeated or continuous misconduct."[88]

Elsewhere the Commission more particularly specify the following acts as justifying detention:—

> (*a*) Wilful refusal or neglect of persons to maintain themselves or their families (although such persons are wholly or in part able to do so), the result of such refusal or neglect being that the persons or their families have become chargeable to the Public Assistance Committees.
>
> (*b*) Wilful refusal on the part of a person receiving assistance to perform the work or to observe the regulations duly prescribed in regard to such assistance.

(c) Wilful refusal to comply with the conditions laid down by the Public Assistance Authority upon which assistance can be obtained, with the result that a person's family thereby become chargeable.

(d) Giving way to gambling, drink, or idleness, with the result that a person or his or her family thereby become chargeable.

They add:—

"The counterparts of the first two of the above offences are already punishable under the Vagrancy Acts, and a third repetition of them renders the offender liable to imprisonment for not more than one year with hard labour. For this punishment we propose to substitute committal to a Detention Colony for any period between six months and three years. This proposal is in general harmony with the recommendations of the Departmental Committee on Vagrancy, and we believe it to be essential to the proper treatment of the ins-and-outs, the work-shy, and the loafer. Moreover, by removing these cases to the care of another authority, the Public Assistance Authority will be enabled to deal more effectively and more hopefully with the better class of workmen applying for assistance."[89]

Again:—

"Stronger measures—particularly detention—should be taken in dealing with the ins-and-outs. Public Assistance Authorities should have power to retain the children of such under their care, and to take proceedings to secure the detention and training of the parents in a suitable institution or colony, until they are prepared to maintain themselves and their families outside.

"Feeble-minded ins-and-outs should be detained in suitable institutions according to the recommendations of the Royal Commission on the Feeble-minded.

"For able-bodied ins-and-outs, who are incapable of maintaining themselves permanently owing to want of discipline, application, or skill, provision should be made by which they would labour according to their strength, and support themselves as far as possible; more varied work might be furnished, and their labour made more productive in supplying the needs of the institution to which they are admitted.

"For those frequenting Public Assistance Institutions who are confirmed drunkards, and persons leading immoral lives there should be power of detention after their incapacity to lead a decent life has been proved.

"Paupers well able to work, *i.e.*, cases of persistent idleness, should be referred to a Detention Colony under the Home Office."[90]

As I have already shown, every one of these social offences is punished by detention and disciplinary treatment in Forced Labour Colonies, variously called, on the Continent. Not only so, but we have seen that the power to commit to these institutions is in many towns exercised by the Poor Law Authorities, either independently of or concurrently with the police and the magistrates.

Beyond recommending that the Detention Colonies should be established by the State, and that the local Public Assistance Authorities should pay for the maintenance of individuals detained by their order or request, the Commission do not go into details, but accept the general conclusions of the Vagrancy Committee.

Not less gratifying than the attitude towards the question of vagrancy of these official investigators is the widespread support which Poor Law Authorities in general have given during the past several years to the repressive policy which is now before the country. The proceedings of the Poor Law Conferences and the Reports of Poor Law Inspectors testify clearly to the new spirit which has come over public opinion. Wherever we look, indeed, signs of changed opinions, abandoned prejudices, and expectations of a new departure are visible. It is not too much to hope and to ask that one of the first steps in the reform of the law of public relief may be the subjection to wholesome systematic restraint of all those parasitic sections of the population which now abuse public and private charity. Only when they cease to obstruct the path of the social reformer will it be possible to view in its true proportions and relationships the momentous question of society's obligation to the unemployed and the helpless poor.

APPENDIX I.

THE CHILDREN ACT, 1908, AND VAGRANTS.

Section 14 (Part II.) of the Children Act, 1908, provides:—

"(1) If any person causes or procures any child or young person or, having the custody or care of a child or young person, allows that child or young person to be in any street, premises, or place for the purpose of begging or receiving alms, or of inducing the giving of alms, whether or not there is any pretence of singing, playing, performing, offering anything for sale, or otherwise, that person shall on summary conviction be liable to a fine not exceeding £25, or alternatively, or in default of payment of such fine, or in addition thereto, to imprisonment, with or without hard labour, for any term not exceeding three months.

"(2) If a person having the custody, charge, or care of a child or young person is charged with an offence under this section, and it is proved that the child or young person was in any street, premises, or place for any purpose as aforesaid, and that the person charged allowed the child or young person to be in the street, premises, or place, he shall be presumed to have allowed him to be in the street, premises, or place for that purpose unless the contrary is proved."

The Act (Section 20), also empowers a constable or any person authorised by a justice to take to a place of safety any child or young person in respect of whom an offence of the kind has been, or there is reason to believe has been, committed, and (Section 21) where a person having the custody, charge, or care of a child or young person has been convicted of committing such an offence in respect of a child or young person, or committed for trial for such offence, a Court of Summary Jurisdiction may order the child or young person to be committed to the care of a relative or other fit person until the age of sixteen years, or for a shorter period, and (Section 22) may make an order for maintenance during such period on the parent of or other person liable to maintain the child or young person, up to the limit of £1 weekly.

Section 118 of the Act provides:—

"(1) If a person habitually wanders from place to place, and takes with him any child above the age of five, he shall, unless he proves that the child is totally exempted from school attendance, or that the child is not, by being so taken with him, prevented from receiving efficient elementary education, be liable on summary conviction to a fine not exceeding, with costs, 20s., and shall, for the purposes of the provisions of this Act relating to the descriptions of children who may be sent to a certified industrial school, be deemed not to be exercising proper guardianship over the child;[91] provided that this provision shall not apply to a child in a canal boat for whose education provision is made under the Canal Boats Act, 1877, as amended by any subsequent enactment.

"(2) Any constable who finds a person wandering from place to place and taking a child with him may, if he has reasonable ground for believing that the person is guilty of an offence under this section, apprehend him without a warrant, and may take the child to a place of safety in accordance with the provisions of Part II. of this Act, and that Part shall apply accordingly as if an offence under this Section were an offence under that Part.

"(3) Without prejudice to the requirements of the Education Acts, 1870 to 1907, as to school attendance, or to proceedings thereunder, this section shall not apply during the months of April to September inclusive to any child whose parent or guardian is engaged in a trade or business of such a nature as to require him to travel from place to place, and who has obtained a certificate of having made not less than 200 attendances at a public elementary school during the months of October to March immediately preceding, and the power of the Board of Education to make regulations with respect to the issue of certificates of due attendance for the purposes of the Education Acts, 1870 to 1907, shall include a power to make regulations as to the issue of certificates of attendance for the purposes of this Section."

Further (Section 75), if children are sent to certified industrial schools under this Section their parents or guardians may be required to contribute towards their maintenance.

APPENDIX II.

SPECIMEN WAY-TICKETS.

I.—WAY-TICKET USED IN GLOUCESTERSHIRE.

Front of Ticket.

Counterfoil.	COUNTY OF GLOUCESTER.					
Pass No.	Pass No._____ Cheltenham Union_____ day of_____ 190_					
Name	Name_____ Occupation_____					
Occupation	Age_____ Height_____ Hair_____ Eyes_____ Complexion_____					
Age	Other distinguishing marks_____					
Height	Came from_____ Final Destination_____					
Hair	Unions on Road.	Arrival. Date. Hour.		Departure. Date. Hour.		Signature of Master.
Eyes						
Complexion						
Other distinguishing marks						
	Date.	Bread Station for the Day.	Bread given.		Hour.	Signature of Constable.
Date of Arrival						
Date of Departure						
Going from						
Final Destination						

Back of Ticket.

CASUAL WARD ADMISSION TICKET.			
No of Pass_____			
Admit_____ as described on the other side as being examined and registered by me.			
Unions.	Relieving Officer's Signature.	Hour of Issue.	Date and Place.
Cheltenham.			

This ticket must be kept, and must be presented to and signed by the Relieving Officer of Vagrants for each Union at which shelter is required.

II.—WAY-TICKET OF THE GERMAN TRAVELLERS' HOSTEL ASSOCIATION (ISSUED IN THE FORM OF A BOOK).

Surname of Owner ....

Christian Name ....

Born........................ 19......

at.......................... District ....

Trade....................... Religious Confession........

Description—

Height...................... Hair........................

Eyes........................ Shape of face...............

Special characteristics ....

OWNER'S AUTOGRAPH SIGNATURE AND PLEDGE.

The undersigned pledges himself by his signature to use this way-ticket according to the regulations, and when using the Stations to observe the travelling and labour regulations printed at the close of this book.

(*Signed*)..

Observations of the Relief Station or Police Authorities regarding papers of identification, extra task work, etc. ....

Issued after production of the following papers of identification:—Removal certificate, insurance receipt card, labour certificate.

(Officer to strike out the words which do not apply).

Issued in the absence of papers of identification as above, after the fulfilment of regulation 3 *d*, and *e*. (Travelling and Labour Regulations).

Place of issue.................. District ....

Date ....

Stamp. Signature of Officer................

Observations of the Station or Police Authorities............

CERTIFICATES OF WORK OR SICKNESS.

The periods and places of employment or of sickness may be briefly noted here on the production of reliable evidence.

From.	To	At	Remarks or Stamp.

TRAVELLING STAMP.

To be entered in the order of the numbers with the date of departure. Where the sojourn was for more than one day, a stamp to be recorded for each day.

Stamp of the Station of Issue.	(Hour)	Departure for
1.	2.	
(Hour) Departure for	(Hour)	Departure for
3.	4.	

APPENDIX III.

BELGIAN LAW OF NOVEMBER 27, 1891, FOR THE REPRESSION OF VAGRANCY AND BEGGING.

Art. 1. For the repression of vagrancy and begging, the Government shall organise institutions of correction under the name of "dépôts de mendicité," "maisons de refuge" and charity schools (écoles de bienfaisance).

Art. 2. The institutions of correction mentioned in the preceding Article shall be exclusively devoted to the confinement of persons whom the judicial authority shall place at the disposal of the Government to be shut up in a "dépôt."

The "maisons de refuge" mentioned in the same Article shall be exclusively devoted to the confinement of persons whom the judicial authority shall place at the disposal of the Government to be confined there, and persons whose confinement is requested by the authority of the commune.

The charity schools shall be devoted to persons who are under eighteen years of age and have been placed by the judicial authority at the disposal of the Government, or whose admission has been applied for by the authority of the commune.

Art. 3. Persons over eighteen years of age, whose confinement in a "maison de refuge" has been applied for by the authority of the commune, shall be admitted when they present themselves voluntarily, provided with the copy of the order of the burgomaster and alderman authorising their admission.

Art. 4. When confinement in a "maison de refuge" has been requested by a communal authority, the costs of maintenance shall be charged to the commune.

Art. 5. Persons under twenty-one years of age confined in the "dépôts" shall be entirely separated from inmates above this age.

Art. 6. Able-bodied persons confined in a "dépôt" or "maison de refuge" shall be kept to the work prescribed in the institution.

They shall receive daily wages, except when withdrawn as a measure of discipline, on which a reserve shall be made in order to form their leaving fund.

The Minister of Justice will fix for the several classes in which the inmates are placed, and according to the labour on which they are employed, the rate of the wages and the amount of the reserve.

The leaving fund shall be paid partly in cash, partly in clothes and tools.

Art. 7. The routine and discipline of the institutions shall be regulated by royal decree.

The inmates may be subjected to solitary confinement.

Art. 8. Every person found in a state of vagrancy shall be arrested and brought before the police tribunal.

Souteneurs shall be treated as vagrants.

The decision of the magistrates concerning souteneurs may be appealed against during the period provided for by the code of criminal instruction.

Art. 9. Any person found begging may be arrested and brought before the police tribunal.

Art. 10. Adult and able-bodied foreigners not residing in Belgium who are found begging or in a state of vagrancy may be at once conducted to the frontier.

Art. 11. Persons arrested under the present law may be provisionally liberated by the Minister of Justice or by the tribunals.

Art. 12. The magistrates shall verify the identity, age, physical and mental condition, and the mode of life of individuals brought before the police tribunal for vagrancy or begging.

Art. 13. They shall place at the disposal of the Government, to be confined in a "dépôt" for at least two years and not more than seven years, able-bodied persons who, instead of working for their living, depend upon charity as professional beggars, and persons who from idleness, drunkenness, or immorality live in a state of vagrancy, and souteneurs.

Art. 14. The correctional courts may put at the disposal of the Government, to be confined in a "dépôt" for not less than a year or more than seven years after the completion of their punishment, vagrants and beggars whom they sentence to imprisonment of less than a year for a breach of the penal law.

Art. 15. The Minister of Justice may liberate persons confined in a "dépôt" where he considers it inexpedient to prolong their detention for the term fixed by the tribunal.

Art. 16. The magistrates may put at the disposal of the Government, to be confined in a "maison de refuge" persons found in a state of vagrancy or begging, without any of the circumstances mentioned in Article 13.

Art. 17. Persons confined in the "maisons de refuge" shall be set free when their leaving fund reaches the amount fixed by the Minister of Justice for the several classes in which the inmates are placed, and according to the trade they follow.

Art. 18. Persons confined in a "maison de refuge" shall not in any case be kept there above a year against their will. The Minister of Justice shall set free any persons confined in a "maison de refuge" whose detention he considers to be no longer necessary.

Art. 19. The Government may at any time conduct to the frontier persons of foreign nationality who have been put at its disposal for detention in a "dépôt" or "maison de refuge."

Art. 20. The managers of the "maisons de refuge" shall give to the inmates, upon their leaving the institution, a certificate of their detention, with attestation of good behaviour, if necessary.

Art. 21. The cost of maintenance of persons confined in a "dépôt" under a decision of the judicial authority shall be borne up to a third part by the commune of their settlement. The remainder shall be divided equally between the State and the province.

The same rule shall apply to the cost of maintenance of able-bodied persons confined in the "maisons de refuge."

When a person confined in a "dépôt" or "maison de refuge" under a decision of the judicial authority has no settlement in Belgium, and his settlement cannot be ascertained, the cost of maintenance to be borne by the commune of settlement under the preceding paragraph shall be borne by the province in which he has been arrested or brought before the court.

In the case of souteneurs the cost shall be borne by the commune in which they were pursuing their practices.

Art. 22. The share falling on the commune of the cost of maintenance of persons confined in the "dépôts" shall be charged to the communal budget.

The share falling on the commune of the cost of maintenance of persons confined in the "maisons de refuge" shall be borne by the almshouses and boards of charity, without prejudice to subsidies by the commune in case of the resources of these institutions being inadequate.

Art. 23. When a person placed at the disposal of the Government to be confined in a "maison de refuge" is declared by the managers to be non-able-bodied, the cost of maintenance, except in the case of injury or sickness occurring during the confinement, shall be borne, as long as the incapacity for work remains, by the commune of his settlement. The managers must give immediate notice of any such case to the commune of settlement.

Art. 24. When the person brought before the police tribunal under Article 8 or Article 9 of the present law is under eighteen years of age, the magistrate, if habitual begging or vagrancy is proved, shall order that he be placed at the disposal of the Government to be confined in a State charity school until he attains his majority.

Art. 25. When a person under the age of sixteen is convicted of having wilfully committed an offence punishable with a police penalty, the court, even in the case of a second offence, shall not sentence him to imprisonment or a fine, but shall record the offence and reprimand the child, or, if the nature and gravity of the offence or the circumstances of the case require it, shall place the child at the disposal of the Government until he comes of age.

Art. 26. The courts and tribunals may, when they sentence to imprisonment a person under the age of eighteen, direct that he shall remain at the disposal of the Government from the expiration of the sentence until he comes of age.

Art. 27. Persons placed at the disposal of the Government under Articles 25 and 26 of the present law shall be confined in a State charity school.

Art. 29. Persons under the age of thirteen at the date of entering a State charity school shall remain, during the whole term of their confinement, entirely separated from persons who enter at a more advanced age.

Similarly, persons entering a State charity school at an age of more than thirteen and less than sixteen years shall remain during the whole term of their confinement separated from persons who enter at a more advanced age.

Art. 30. Persons placed at the disposal of the Government under Articles 24, 25 and 26 of the present law, or Article 72 of the Penal Code, may, after confinement in a State charity school, be placed in apprenticeship with a farmer or artisan; they may also with the assent of their parents or guardian be placed in a public or private institution for instruction.

Art. 31. Persons confined in State charity schools may be returned conditionally to their parents or guardian by direction of the Minister of Justice, if the parents or guardian afford sufficient guarantees of good character and are in a position to take care of the child.

Art. 32. Persons returned conditionally to their parents or guardian, as provided in the preceding Article, may, until coming of age, be re-instated in a State charity school, by direction of the Minister of Justice, if it is considered that their residence with their parents or guardian has become dangerous to their morals. For the purposes of the rule established by Article 29 of the present law, they shall be deemed to have been placed at the disposal of the Government at the date on which they were re-instated.

Art. 34. The cost of maintenance and education of persons placed in State charity schools shall be charged to the State as regards one-half; and, as regards the other half, to the commune of settlement if they have been placed at the disposal of the Government by a decision of the judicial authority, or to the commune which has applied for their admission.

When a person confined in a State charity school under a decision of the judicial authority has no place of settlement in Belgium and when his place of settlement cannot be ascertained, the cost of maintenance and education charged to the commune of settlement by the preceding paragraph, shall be borne by the province in which he has been arrested or brought before the magistrate.

Art. 35. The cost of maintenance and education of children placed at the disposal of the Government under Articles 25 and 26 shall be borne by the State.

Art. 37. The King will fix annually the price per day of maintenance in the State charity schools, in the "maisons de refuge" and the "dépôts."

Art. 38. The cost of relief given in execution of the present law may be recovered from the persons relieved or from those liable for their maintenance. It may also be recovered from those who are responsible for the injury or illness which necessitates the relief.

Art. 39. The following are liable to imprisonment from eight days to three months:—

> (1) A person who habitually causes a child under sixteen years of age to beg; and
>
> (2) A person who procures a child under sixteen years of age or a cripple for the purpose of being used to excite public pity.

In the case of a second offence the penalty may be doubled.

Art. 42. The present law shall come into force on January 1, 1892.

APPENDIX IV.

REGULATIONS OF THE BERLIN (RUMMELSBURG) LABOUR HOUSE.

(1) The inmates are required to conform with the present regulations, and always to yield punctual obedience to all officers of the establishment, as their superiors, and to the military guard.

(2) After the execution of orders given to them, inmates are only allowed to offer criticisms thereupon or make complaints in a modest manner. Complaints and wishes of any kind shall be brought before the Director of the establishment, to which end the inmate must request his sectional overseer to take him to the Director. Every inmate may address the Director or Inspector, and bring to their notice complaints and wishes, in the course of their walks round. Conscious misrepresentations regarding officers of the establishment or the military guard will be punished.

(3) The inmates shall live together in peace and quiet, none interrupting another in his work, but rather by industry, order, and decent moral behaviour encouraging each other to reformation of life and setting each other a good example. Conversation upon past misdemeanours may under no circumstances take place; nor may one inmate reproach another with any crime which he may have committed, or with his past course of life, abuse or threaten him, or in any way physically misuse him. No inmate may avenge himself for a wrong done to him by another inmate.

(4) It is forbidden to climb upon the windows, to soil or write upon the walls, to defile the landings, stairs, etc., to sing, shout, whistle, play cards, dice, or other games of chance, to be in possession of money, writing materials (paper, ink, pen, pencil), matches, knives, cord, rope, iron tools, to smoke or chew, drink spirit, or secretly obtain spirit. The inmates may not sell, exchange, give, or lend articles of any kind. Articles found must be at once given up to the overseer.

(5) In the morning at the time prescribed in the regulations (Section 26) every inmate must carefully wash his face, neck, and hands, and comb his hair, in the place assigned to him. In general every inmate must continually observe the greatest cleanliness in regard both to his body and clothing, and to all the rooms of the establishment. All deliberate or malicious damage to the property of the establishment or of inmates, besides entailing punishment, must be made good.

(6) Any inmate who conceals an illness from which he is suffering is punishable, equally with one who feigns illness. Every trace of vermin on

body, bed, clothing, or elsewhere must immediately be notified to the overseer.

(7) The quitting of a place of work or other assigned position unnecessarily, or without permission, disturbances of quiet and order, the soiling or tearing down of notices, the use of indecent language, all immodest behaviour, and all swearing and abuse will be punished.

(8) During divine service, which every inmate who is not formally excused must attend, the utmost quiet must be observed. Disturbances during prayers in the dining room and during divine service will be emphatically punished.

(9) Immediately after the closing of the dining room in the evening every inmate shall unclothe himself to his shirt, place his clothing in an orderly way in the place assigned to him, and go to bed, which he may not leave until the general signal for rising is given in the morning, except, etc.

(10) The greatest precaution must be used with fire and light, and every unauthorised or careless use of the same, causing or threatening injury to the building or its effects, will be severely punished.

(11) Should a signal be given in the night that fire has broken out, every inmate must at once leave his bed, dress himself, and quietly await orders. Every mischievous or malicious disturbance on such occasions will be punished with special severity.

(12) Every attempt to evade control or at concealment at locking up time will be punished. Violent attempts will be punished by the criminal court. Any one who escapes from the establishment or from outside work will be punished with detention on his recapture and anyone taking his uniform when escaping will be prosecuted for theft.

(13) Whoever foments a conspiracy amongst the inmates will either be punished for breach of discipline or be handed over to the police.

(14) Whoever wishes to write a letter must obtain the Director's permission. Letter-writing takes place, as a rule, on Sunday. The clandestine writing, despatch, and receipt of letters is strictly prohibited. Letters received and those to be despatched must first be examined by the authorised officials. All letters received after being read, are to be deposited in the administrative office, there to be put away with other documents referring to the persons to whom they relate.

(15) All intercourse with strangers appearing in the establishment, for whatever purpose, and with the military guard, is forbidden, as are also speaking, beckoning, etc., between male and female inmates. Strangers, as well as members of the municipal or other authority visiting the

establishment, may only speak with inmates with the permission of the overseers present.

(16) Visits to inmates may only be made by near relatives, and such persons as have to discuss business, and then only with the permission of the Director, and in the presence of an officer. Visitors must furnish proof of their identity and of their *bona-fide* business with the inmates concerned. Conversation between the inmates may only take place in a language known to the attendant officer. Every abuse of the permission to visit an inmate will entail the immediate removal of the visitor and punishment of the inmate according to the circumstances of the case.

(17) Every inmate is required to perform, without demur, and to the best of his ability, the work allotted to him, either inside or outside the establishment. As a rule, all inmates have to work on weekdays an equal number of hours, and to perform in that time a task proportionate to their capacity, the completion of which, however, does not exempt them from working to the end of the usual time. The administration may, however, under certain circumstances curtail the duration of the daily hours of work, and the extent of the task in individual cases. Anyone who, owing to idleness or negligence, fails to perform his allotted task, or who in general works slothfully or negligently, will be punished. No inmate may, without permission, allow his work to be done for him by another or do another's work.

(18) No work is done on Sundays and Christian festivals. Prisoners of the Jewish religion may, at their request, be exempted from work on the Sabbath and the Jewish high festivals:—Feast of Weeks, New Year, Feast of Expiation, Feast of Tabernacles, and the first two and the last two days of the Passover; in that event they may, on the order of the Director, be employed in noiseless work as Sundays and the Christian festivals.

(19) The proceeds of the work done by the inmates on the order of the administration belong to the Municipality of Berlin, and are paid into the treasury of the establishment. The extra-pay paid to the inmates by employers is divided into two equal parts, of which one is placed at the inmate's disposal for the purchase of extra food, the payment of postage, and other necessary expenses, during his detention, while the other accumulates as savings until his discharge.

(20) Every inmate must deposit his tools and implements in an orderly manner at the assigned place at the close of work; he may not take anything with him from the workshop.

(21) When going to work, church, meals, exercise, or reporting himself, and when going to bed, the inmates must always be completely and orderly dressed. The men's work aprons must always be left in the workshop....

(22) The extra articles of food which inmates are allowed to purchase out of their earnings are given out on Saturday. Like all barter, the exchange of these extras and gifts of the same are strictly prohibited.

(23) Sick persons are required to follow strictly the prescriptions given to them by the doctor. Anyone who feels unwell must report himself to the sectional overseer. Visits to the doctor unaccompanied by the overseer are prohibited.

(24) Even inmates whose discharge is due are required to follow the regulations strictly while in the establishment, and until they are discharged. Should they be allowed in exceptional cases after completing their sentences to remain for a further period in the establishment they may not abuse the permission by executing commissions for other inmates.

(25) All male inmates must have their hair cut short and their beard shaven, but in the event of objection on the ground of religious scruples or health the Director shall decide.

(26) Offences against these regulations, in so far as they do not give rise to judicial proceedings, are punished as breaches of discipline. Disciplinary powers are exercised by the Director. The following disciplinary punishments are awarded: (1) Reprimand; (2) withdrawal of permission to receive visits; (3) withdrawal of permission to write letters and to receive them before discharge; (4) withdrawal of permission to dispose of the part of an inmate's earnings set apart for the purchase of food extras, etc.; (5) partial or complete withdrawal of wages; (6) withdrawal of permission to take outdoor exercise; (7) curtailment of rations; (8) detention; (9) close detention. For the momentary curbing of physical resistance or violent outbreaks and shrieking, chains, chair, and straight-jacket may be used. The isolation of an inmate which may be ordered by the Director in the interest of discipline, pending the decision of the matter at issue, is not regarded as punishment. In suitable cases the Director is empowered to propose to the State Police Authority the prolongation of the term of detention.

FOOTNOTES:

[1] An Act of 1495 (11 Henry VII.) ordered local authorities to search for all "vagaboundes, idell and suspecte persones lyvyng suspeciously," to put them in the stocks for three days, giving them bread and water only, and then to turn them out of the town or township; failing their departure they were to be put in the stocks for six days more, yet still they had to go.

An Act of 1530 (22 Henry VIII.), said in the preamble to be due to the increase of vagrancy, and consequently of crime and disorder, enjoined whipping as an alternative to the stocks, and extended the statute to fortune tellers; a second offence by the latter was made punishable by whipping on two successive days, three hours in the pillory, and the loss of one ear.

An Act of 1535 (27 Henry VIII.) made further provision for the able-bodied and infirm poor, but meted severer punishment to the ruffler, sturdy vagabond, or valiant beggar, who on a second apprehension might have the upper part of the right ear cut off, and on conviction at Quarter Sessions of "wandering, loitering, and idleness," might be sentenced to death as felons.

The preamble of the Act of 1547 (1 Edward VI.) lamented that earlier legislation on the subject of vagrancy "hath not had that success which hath byn wished, partelie by folishe pitie and mercie of them which shoulde have seen the said godlie lawes executed, partelie by the perverse nature and longe accustumed idlenes of the parsons given to loytringe." Accordingly this Act provided that those who would not work nor "offer themself to labour with anny that will take them according to their facultie, and yf no man otherwise will take them doo not offer themself to worke for meate and drynck," also those who ran away from their employment, should be taken as vagabonds before two justices of the peace, who might order them to be branded on the breast with a V and "adjudge the said parsone living so idelye to such presentour to be his slave" for two years. Should the slave run away during the two years he was liable on recapture to be branded on cheek and forehead with an S, and be adjudged a slave for ever, while to run away a second time was felony punishable with death. If private persons failed to set the law in motion the local justices were to do so.

In 1572 (14 Elizabeth) a law was passed enjoining that sturdy beggars found begging should be "grevouslye whipped, and burnte through the gristle of the right eare with a hot iron," unless some one would take them into service for one year; a second offence was to be treated as a felony unless some one would take them into service for two years; and a third offence was made felony without benefit of clergy.

An amending Act of 1597 omitted the provisions as to branding and earmarking, but branding with a R in the left shoulder was reintroduced for incorrigible or dangerous rogues in 1603 (1 James I.). (Branding continued to be legal until 1713.) The Act of 1597 also enjoined banishment for dangerous rogues who refused to reform their lives, and an Order in Council of 1603 particularised the countries to which they should be sent—East and West Indies, France, Germany, Spain, and the Netherlands. The same power to banish was reasserted by a law of 1662, the destination being now "any of the English plantations."

One of the most sensible of the earlier repressive laws was that of 1702-3 (2 & 3 Anne) for the increase of seamen and encouragement of navigation, which empowered justices of the peace to send rogues and vagabonds to "Her Majesty's Service at Sea."

[2] Report, Vol. I., p. 9.

[3] "Casual pauper" is defined in the Pauper Inmates Discharge and Regulation Act of 1871 as "any destitute wayfarer or wanderer applying for or receiving relief" in the casual wards.

[4] "Annual Report" for 1908, p. 10.

[5] Annual Report of the Local Government Board, 1902-3, p. 57.

[6] *Ibid.*, Report of Mr. P. H. Bagenal, p. 147.

[7] Report of Departmental Committee on Vagrancy, Vol. I., p. 16.

[8] "In point of distribution through the country vagrancy is found to cling to the Metropolis and its neighbourhood, and to the manufacturing and coal and iron mining districts; it follows also the track of the navvy when any new works of importance are in progress." Report of Poor Law Commission, Vol. II., pp. 161, 162.

[9] Report of Vagrancy Committee, Vol. I., p. 22.

[10] Report of Vagrancy Committee, Vol. I., p. 1.

[11] Annual Report of the Local Government Board, 1906-7, pp. 292, 293.

[12] Report, Vol. III., p. 507.

[13] Annual Report of the Local Government Board for 1902-3; report of Mr. H. Preston Thomas upon the counties of Cornwall, Devon, &c., pp. 164, 165.

[14] Mr. G. A. F. Hervey, writing of Norfolk and Suffolk. Report for 1902-3, p. 67.

[15] Mr. G. Walsh, reporting on Leicestershire, Lincolnshire, etc. Report for 1907, p. 332.

[16] Mr. R. J. Dansey, writing of the Midland Counties. Report for 1908, p. 71.

[17] Mr. G. Walsh, writing of the counties of Leicester, Lincoln, Nottingham, etc. Report for 1908, pp. 77, 78.

[18] Report, Vol. I., pp. 32, 33.

[19] *Ibid.*, Vol. I., p. 28.

[20] Report, Vol. I., p. 30.

[21] Mr. J. S. Davy. Report of the Local Government Board for 1902-3, p. 57.

[22] Mr. J. W. Thompson. Report for 1908, p. 43.

[23] Mr. A. B. Lowry, Local Government Board Report for 1908, p. 82.

[24] Annual Report of the Local Government Board, 1908; report of Mr. G. Walsh for Leicestershire, Lincolnshire, etc., pp. 78, 79.

[25] Annual Report of the Local Government Board, 1902-3, p. 57.

[26] Mr. P. H. Bagenal in Annual Report of the Local Government Board, 1906, p. 337.

[27] Report for the year ended March, 1905.

[28] Report on Small-pox in relation to Vagrancy in England and Wales during the year 1903, by Dr. H. E. Armstrong, Newcastle.

[29] Annual Report for 1908, p. 79.

[30] The passages in which the question of child vagrancy was dealt with ten years ago have been modified, owing to the passing of the Children Act, 1908, yet important though the provisions of this statute are, they are no final solution. Extracts from the Act are given in Appendix I., pp. 251-253.

[31] Report, Vol I., p. 42.

[32] Annual Report of Local Government Board, 1907; report of Mr. J. S. Oxley, Inspector for the Metropolis, etc.

[33] Evidence before Poor Law Commission, Q. 16,686.

[34] Report of Local Government Board for 1907, p. 312.

[35] Report, Vol. II., p. 278.

[36] Report, Vol. II., p. 279.

[37] The Poor Law Act of 1899, amending an Act of 1889, provides that a child maintained by a Board of Guardians may be taken into the guardians' control until it reaches the age of eighteen years, the guardians acquiring all rights over it meanwhile, if the child has been deserted by its parent, if the guardians think that the parent, by reason of mental deficiency or vicious habits or mode of life, is unfit to have control of the child, if the parent is unable to perform his or her parental duties by reason of being under sentence of penal servitude or of being detained under the Inebriates Act, 1898, or the parent has been sentenced to imprisonment in respect of any offence against any of his or her children, or the parent is permanently bed-ridden or disabled and is an inmate of the workhouse and consents to the guardians so acting, and if both the parents (or in the case of an illegitimate child the mother of the child), are dead.

[38] The figures for six years are as follows:—1902, 2,832; 1903, 3,187; 1904, 3,235; 1905, 3,266; 1906, 3,095; 1907, 3,041.

[39] Qs. 3281, 3347, 3358-9.

[40] "Berliner Lokalanzeiger," July, 1909.

[41] "Berliner Lokalanzeiger," July, 1909.

[42] "Liberty," Chapter IV.

[43] I take the following from a newspaper (January 1, 1904):—"At the Grantham Borough Police Court two vagrants, were sent to gaol for twenty-one days, with hard labour, for refusing to work whilst inmates of the casual ward at the Grantham Workhouse. One of the magistrates said this appeared to be the only way to deal with the question, but the Chief Constable remarked that such men were too comfortable in prison, and that was the reason why they liked going there so much. The master at the workhouse said he heard two others wish they were going with them to gaol."

[44] The terms Detention Colony and Labour House are here, for convenience, used synonymously, though strictly speaking, a colony is an establishment in the country to which land for farming and for improvement is attached, while the Labour House may be located in a town.

[45] Report of Vagrancy Committee, Vol. I., p. 67.

[46] *See* pp. 195-197.

[47] The principal offences committed by these guests were: Larceny, frauds, and receiving stolen property, 97; begging and sleeping out, 18; burglary, housebreaking, etc., 25; frequenting public places with intent to commit felony, etc., 11; sexual offences, indecency, etc., 8; brothel-keeping, 50;

prostitution, 19; living on prostitutes' earnings, 25; and wounding, assaults, drunkenness, etc., 18.

[48] The Prison Commissioners (Report for 1903, p. 119), estimate that the annual net cost per head, after deducting the value of work done, is £22 11s. in local and £29 in convict prisons, exclusive of all charge for buildings.

[49] For a description of Merxplas, *see* pp. 104-132.

[50] Statute of 27 Henry VIII., c. 25.

[51] That this principle was not always the fetish it has become is shown by the following extract from Dr. Burn's "History of the Poor Law," published in 1764:—"But how shall begging be restrained, which by a kind of prescriptive claim hath so long been accustomed to triumph above the laws? All sorts of severities, it appears, have been enacted against vagrants; and yet they wander still. Nevertheless, one would hope the disease is not past all remedy. If it is, let us cease the unequal contention, and submissively give up our fortunes to the next that comes with a pass, and tells us a justice of the peace hath so ordered it; but let beggars and vagrants be doing. There is one infallible way to put an end to all this, and the easiest in the world, which consists merely in a non-feasance. Give them nothing. If none were to give, none would beg, and the whole mystery and craft would be at an end in a fortnight. Let the laws continue if you please to apprehend and punish the mendicants; but let something also be done effectually against those who encourage them. If the principal is punished it is not reasonable the accessory should go free. In order to which, let all who relieve a common beggar be subject to a penalty."

[52] In my evidence before the Departmental Committee on Vagrancy, I fully described the hostel and way ticket system which has for many years been in successful operation in Germany, and the same information was given by Mr. H. Preston Thomas regarding the more recent Swiss system. *See also* Chap. X. (pp. 212-228), of the present Volume.

[53] Mr. J. W. Thompson, in Annual Report for 1908, p. 42.

[54] For the full text of the law see Appendix III., pp. 258-263.

[55] Report of the Vagrancy Committee adopted by the Court of Quarter Sessions (Lincolnshire, Parts of Lindsey) on Friday, October 23, 1903.

[56] The Report of the Lindsey Quarter Sessions Committee on Vagrancy says that the original cost to the Government of the Merxplas estate was £32,000.

[57] In winter coffee is distributed immediately after the bread.

[58] On Saturday work ends an hour earlier.

[59] Biedermann, "Deutschland im 18 ten Jahrhundert," Vol. I., p. 401.

[60] "Statistik der zum Ressort des Königlich Preussischen Ministeriums des Innern gehörenden Strafanstalten und Gefängnisse und der Korrigenden für das Rechnungsjahr 1903," pp. xx-xxii.

[61] The proportion in 1869 was 73 per cent.; in 1895, 52 per cent.; in 1896, 52·6 per cent.; in 1897, 49·1 per cent.; in 1898, 45·7 per cent.; in 1900, 40·4 per cent.; in 1901, 37 per cent.; in 1902, 32·8 per cent.; and in 1903, 27·2 per cent.

[62] *Ibid.*

[63] A portion of this chapter was published in the *Fortnightly Review* of February, 1907.

[64] The full Regulations of the Rummelsburg Labour House appear as an Appendix on pp. 263-267.

[65] There are now four such Labour Colonies in Switzerland.

[66] "The German Workman: a Study in National Efficiency," pp, 293-301 (London: P. S. King & Son, 1906).

[67] "Der Wanderer," 1909, p. 355.

[68] *Ibid.*, p. 351.

[69] Report of the Vice-Regal Commission on Poor Law Reform in Ireland, Vol. I., p. 55.

[70] *Ibid.*, Vol. I., p. 58.

[71] *Ibid.*, Vol. I., p. 55.

[72] Report of the Departmental Committee on Vagrancy, Vol. I., p. 34.

[73] *Ibid.*, p. 59.

[74] Report of the Departmental Committee on Vagrancy, Vol. I., pp. 51 and 53-54.

[75] *Ibid.*, p. 66.

[76] *Ibid.*, p. 70.

[77] Report of the Departmental Committee on Vagrancy, Vol. I., p. 80.

[78] *Ibid.*, p. 87.

[79] *Ibid.*, p. 77.

[80] "There are no means of estimating approximately the number of tramps who might properly be committed to labour colonies, and it is even more

impossible to estimate how many would actually be committed if provision were made by law for the purpose. The result of any Government Department undertaking to supply sufficient accommodation for all the vagrants committed by the magistrates would either be that the accommodation would be wholly inadequate for the requirements, or, as is perhaps more probable, that public money would be wasted in establishing and fitting up institutions in which, for at all events some years, the provision made would be altogether disproportionate to the number of inmates....

"There is another consideration to which we attach great weight, and it is that labour colonies established by the State would inevitably have to be all of the same type, and we have at present no sufficient knowledge to determine exactly what that type should be."—Report, Vol. I., pp. 75.

[81] *See* pp. 89-91.

[82] Report of Vagrancy Committee, Vol. I., p. 82.

[83] *Ibid.*, Vol. I., p. 34.

[84] *See* Chap. III., pp 96-103.

[85] Report of Vagrancy Committee, Vol. I., pp. 43 and 49.

[86] For the rules of the Westphalian system of Relief Stations, *see* Chap. IX., p. 212-215, and for text of way-tickets, *see* Appendix II., p. 254-257.

[87] Report of Vagrancy Committee, Vol. I., pp. 48, 49.

[88] Majority Report, Vol. II., pp. 544, 545.

[89] *Ibid.*, Vol. II., p. 549.

[90] Majority Report, Vol. II., pp. 282, 283.

[91] *Inter alia*, children "found wandering, and not having any home or settled place of abode or visible means of subsistence," or "found wandering and having no parent or guardian, or a parent or guardian who does not exercise proper guardianship" (Section 58, *b*).

Milton Keynes UK
Ingram Content Group UK Ltd.
UKHW030740071024
449371UK00006B/688